American Playwrights
on Drama

FIRST EDITION SEPTEMBER 1965
SECOND PRINTING AUGUST 1966

Manufactured in the United States of America
by The Colonial Press Inc.

American Playwrights

on Drama

EDITED BY HORST FRENZ , 1912

A Dramabook
HILL and WANG · New York

Contents

47334

Introduction

THERE IS NO LACK of books and critical essays on the American theatre and individual playwrights, but this is the only collection of essays by twentieth-century American playwrights. Here, they discuss the various problems of the American theatre and give their impressions of the contemporary state of the drama in this country. At times, they speak about themselves, their experiences, their plans, and their writing habits; at others, they delve into the idiosyncrasies of the American theatre and express their attitude toward Broadway; occasionally, they discuss more general matters, such as verse in drama or drama versus fiction.

The American theatre is over two hundred years old, but a distinctly native drama has been slow in developing. To be sure, there was from the beginning a steady and growing concern with specifically American subjects and characters, as may be seen from the Indian and Yankee plays, plays about the frontier and slavery, plays dealing with the American Revolution and later with the Civil War. However, no truly outstanding American playwright emerged prior to the twentieth century. There are several reasons for this. During the nineteenth century, the American drama—like the drama in England—was handicapped by a certain cosmopolitanism, for it borrowed widely and freely from foreign playwrights. Furthermore, the actor captured the imagination of the public and ruled supreme, making it almost impossible for the author to assert himself. Finally, as in Europe, profound changes in the conception of man and his universe necessitated a new stagecraft and new theatre techniques and called for experimentation before the drama could free itself from popular theatrical conventions.

In our century the situation has changed. It is true that Eugene O'Neill and Robinson Jeffers revived the classical myths, that Maxwell Anderson's essay on the essence of tragedy is based on the *Poetics* of Aristotle, that Archibald MacLeish tried his hand at a modern version of the mystery play, that Thornton Wilder went back to Nestroy and Oxenford, that Elmer Rice and Paul Green adopted techniques of the expressionists, and that Edward Albee has followed the basic concepts of the French Theatre of the Absurd. But these European influences are subordinate; they have been absorbed. Much of the work of these writers is American in substance and spirit. The American theatre reflects the variety of the American scene; it ranges from folk elements to decadence, from the description of almost primitive conditions to the height of sophistication. O'Neill's characters have grown on American soil; Arthur Miller's salesman is a typical American phenomenon; Wilder represents the life of an American family; Tennessee Williams' characters are genuine Southerners, William Inge's come from the Middle West, Albee's are "absurd" Americans. Still, the frequent occurrence of the names of Strindberg, Ibsen, Chekhov, Shaw, and Yeats in these essays shows the interest American playwrights have taken in the development of European drama. O'Neill was always aware that Strindberg first inspired him to write plays and influenced him profoundly. Miller has openly declared himself a disciple of Ibsen; he has repeatedly stated that Ibsen has still much to say to us and that he follows Ibsen in looking upon the stage as the place for a discussion of the problems of modern man. Williams has expressed his fondness for Lorca and pointed out that like many other contemporary American writers he has learnt much from Chekhov, especially in regard to characterization.

Modern American drama was born in Provincetown, where, in 1915, there gathered a small group of theatre enthusiasts. In an abandoned building on the waterfront and later in Greenwich Village they put on dramatic pieces by young American playwrights (O'Neill among them) and also staged plays by Strindberg and other European writers. The close contact with an experimental theatre was a useful experience for a would-be playwright. O'Neill found support and encouragement within the group.

O'Neill enjoyed experimenting and he made new and unexpected use of such conventional devices as the aside, the soliloquy, and the mask. At times he experimented even during the writing of a play. In an early draft of *Mourning Becomes Electra,* for instance, the characters wore masks; later O'Neill changed his mind and gave his characters a masklike appearance. After the première of the play, however, he said that he should have made freer use of masks in that play and in other works of his. O'Neill's work diary is an important document for the understanding of the development of a dramatist who has explored the interrelation of material and ideal values, of appearance and reality, of wish and fulfillment, and who has portrayed characters of great psychological complexity.

O'Neill never founded a school, and the constant experimenting and the frequent change of style, which are so noticeable in his work, characterize the work of other American dramatists as well. Wilder was radical in his rejection of the peephole stage. O'Neill had high hopes for the use of masks, for, as he points out in his essay "Memoranda on Masks" (which has been impossible to reprint here): "One's outer life passes in solitude haunted by the masks of others; one's inner life passes in a solitude hounded by the masks of oneself." O'Neill considered masks a symbol of inner reality and thought not only that they had more dramatic potential than the face of an actor but that they stimulated the imagination of the spectators and made them share more deeply in the action of a play and its characters. Like Wilder in his essays, he referred to the Asiatic theatre and in particular to the no plays and the Chinese opera. Wilder stressed the empty stage of that theatre, which demands of the spectator that he re-create the reality of the scene in his imagination, helped only by the dramatist's words and the suggestive acting of the players. (This style of acting, just as the use of masks, puts of course equally high demands on the actor.) In several of his plays Wilder has used an empty stage and few props in an attempt to free himself from the usual conventions of

space and time. He does not regard himself as "an innovator" but as "a rediscoverer of forgotten goods." Like
O'Neill, he has indubitably helped formulate a fresh and
exciting approach to the theatre. His unconventional use
of traditional devices has shown the road to a theatre of
the future; he may well have made it easier for such
younger dramatists as Albee and Kopit to succeed.

On the other hand, Wilder and O'Neill differ fundamentally in their basic attitudes toward life. Alan Downer
has defined this difference: "To Wilder the American
dream is a recoverable reality; if O'Neill is among the dis-
enchanted, he at least knows the reality of what has been
lost." In *Our Town* and his one-act plays Wilder has shown
that even the common events of daily life are dramatically
significant. *The Skin of Our Teeth* bears witness to his firm
belief in the continuity of human life despite the cata-
strophic visitations of history. Wilder's qualified optimism
and simple wisdom are his most impressive characteristics.

Since the end of the war Tennessee Williams and Arthur
Miller have become prominent on the American stage.
Both deal predominantly with American subject matter
and have treated it at times with astonishing frankness.
Both dramatists look for their heroes among the hurt, the
desperate, and the weak. But the similarity of their themes
should not obscure the difference of their approach. Kenneth Tynan, in *Curtains,* has said that Miller stresses the
"dynamic quality of fact" whereas Williams' plays have
the "static quality of dream." Miller, Tynan continues, describes the active present, the "male preserve wherein history is shaped," Williams the past and future, "nostalgia
and hope," the sufferings of complex female characters.
This distinction leads to a further contrast: Tennessee
Williams thinks in individual and psychological terms,
Arthur Miller in social and sociological terms. One need
only think of Miller's essay "The Shadows of the Gods,"
in which he deals with a common theme on the contemporary American stage, the dilemma of young people in
revolt against an inadequate society. Miller uses Williams'
Cat on a Hot Tin Roof as an example to show that Williams' vision is too narrow because he treats only the
personal problems of his characters and ignores the social

forces that underlie them. Miller believes that the American theatre must transcend a purely emotional perspective and attempt an evaluation of the world.

To a considerable extent, Miller echoed some of the ideas expressed by the writers of social revolt, particularly active in the late twenties and the thirties and including such playwrights as Clifford Odets, John Howard Lawson, Irwin Shaw, and Lillian Hellman. Lawson, best known for his *Processional,* has represented these ideas most forcefully in his *Theory and Technique of Playwriting,* which argues that social conflict is the essence of drama. In its insistence on the importance of the effects of social and economic forces on the characters of a drama, Lawson's book, from which the chapter entitled "The Social Framework" is reprinted here, shows much similarity with the content of Miller's essays. To Lawson as well as to Miller, Ibsen's work shows how inevitably social necessity determines the course of action in drama.

The interest in psychology is perhaps the most important phenomenon of contemporary American drama, and it reflects the intellectual confusion of the last decades. The recurrent themes are often the problems of young people who rebel against the authority of their parents or society, or the problems of adults who escape from the present to childhood memories or wish fulfillments. *Come Back, Little Sheba* illustrates this point. In his essay "The Schizophrenic Wonder," Inge has described the psychological motives of his two main characters, a married couple who reflect glumly on the vanished and never-realized happiness of their youth and are "looking tentatively in the future for something to replace" this youthful happiness. Both are lovable human beings, as the author says, but certainly not tragic heroes. Inge, who added life to the theatre of the fifties with several realistic dramas but who in his later plays did not match the achievement of *Come Back, Little Sheba,* denied expressly that he wanted to write a tragedy.

Elmer Rice in his essay on psychoanalytic drama comes to the conclusion that such drama simply cannot reach tragic status, an opinion that Miller echoes in his essay on tragedy and extends to drama that is merely sociologically oriented. These remarks may apply to modern drama in general, but it has been said that the American theatre in particular could not produce a tragedy. There are several reasons for such an assumption. An interesting explanation appeared under the title of "Untragic America" in *Life* Magazine on the occasion of the première of O'Neill's *The Iceman Cometh* in 1946.

After discussing Aristotle's theory of tragedy the anonymous author of this essay expresses his conviction that an American tragedy is impossible for two reasons. First, the democratic axiom that all men are equal prevents the Americans from having as much respect for a dramatic character as the Athenians had for Oedipus or the Elizabethans for Lear. Second, the optimistic belief in progress has replaced the older conviction that man is sinful and is not the master of his fate. A sense of tragedy, so the author argues, cannot develop as long as Americans cling to these two beliefs, reject the existence of higher powers, and consider all problems as soluble. This popular explanation coincides to a certain degree with similar ideas about modern tragedies, which Rice and Inge suggest in their essays and O'Neill in his work diary.

And yet, there are American playwrights who have deliberately attempted to write tragedies, among them O'Neill's contemporary, Maxwell Anderson. After plays in prose Anderson published historical tragedies in verse and a number of verse plays, such as *Winterset,* which treat contemporary subjects. *Winterset,* Anderson's most important tragedy, was clearly constructed in accordance with the dramatic theories that Anderson developed in "The Essence of Tragedy" as an extension of Aristotle's remarks on "recognition." This attempt to write a modern tragedy in *verse* aroused considerable interest in *Winterset.* It has frequently been pointed out that the problem of tragedy is primarily a problem of language, and some critics have refused to accord *Mourning Becomes Electra* the status of a tragedy because its language is unpoetic. On the other hand, it has been argued that a tragedy dealing with common people should be written in everyday prose. Anderson objects to this argument maintaining that prose is the language of information, not of emotion, and hence an unfit instrument for the ambitious dramatist. T. S. Eliot and Archibald MacLeish also have recognized that there are areas of emotions that are simply not accessible to prose. MacLeish goes further in his defense of poetic drama and shows that the demand for prose, because it is realistic, is not based on any dramatic necessity but only on the conventional expectation of the audience, which wants to experience the illusion of reality on the stage. He shows that this convention is by no means unalterable. According to MacLeish, the dramatist's true taste consists in creating the "illusion of the real," and for this purpose poetry is often superior to prose. MacLeish sees the chief problem of the dramatic poet as that of reconciling the language of modern poetry with the requirements of drama. Anderson usually wrote a stylized prose that changed to poetry in scenes of emotional intensity. When *Winterset* was produced on Broadway in the mid-thirties, other theatres were playing *Murder in the Cathedral*. A comparison was inevitable and revealed Eliot as the greater poet, Anderson as the more skillful dramatic craftsman. Critics pointed out rightly that a truly great poetic drama demands both fine poetry and skillful theatre.

In some respects Archibald MacLeish, who had proved the dramatic power of his verse in several radio plays of the thirties, has come close to this goal in his modern Everyman play, *J. B.* The language ranges from doggerel to the lofty words of the Book of Job, and the stylistic tensions add substantially to the dramatic tension. Next to MacLeish, Robinson Jeffers has doubtless made the most significant contributions to American verse drama. He took his subjects from Greek tragedy but, unlike O'Neill, refrained from dramatizing them in a modern setting. Nevertheless, language and interpretation of the myth in *The Tower Beyond Tragedy,* for instance, reveal the unmistakable spirit of a modern writer.

Tragedy has been a favorite topic of discussion with the American dramatists from O'Neill to Miller, but little has been written about comedy. And yet the modern American theatre has produced many good comedies. Perhaps the precepts for a successful comedy are too simple to arouse much discussion: a fast-moving action, witty dialogue, and preposterous situations. S. N. Behrman, however, represents the much rarer type of high comedy, which he discusses in one of the essays in this book. Behrman combines, in his best work, intelligence, wit, and tolerance toward human weaknesses. The effect of his comedies derives largely from sprightly dialogue and the skillful contrast of sharply delineated characters, who are at times unusually articulate and pursue even trivial matters with mock seriousness. More recently, the playwrights of the Absurd have been experimenting with such comic devices as conventional clichés, everyday platitudes, and nonsense words or phrases, occasionally with extremely startling effects. Their theatre can become, in Albee's words, "free-swinging, bold, iconoclastic, and often wildly, wildly funny."

Paul Green is chiefly known for his symphonic dramas. By using pantomime, dance, music, and choruses, he has enlarged the possibilities of the ordinary stage. Green's plays have nearly all been written for outdoor theatres. He has been active in spreading the idea of this kind of theatre and advancing the cause of local theatres, and has frequently written on the value of popular theatre. Green's work has, more than once, shown his deep and sympathetic interest in Southern Negro life. There have been other American playwrights who have dealt with Negroes as major characters, particularly O'Neill in *The Emperor Jones* and *All God's Chillun Got Wings* and Marc Connelly in *The Green Pastures*. However, very few Negro playwrights have emerged, and the reasons for this are put forth frankly in the essay by Lorraine Hansberry, whose early death brought to an end the career of a promising and gifted playwright.

The essays pay a great deal of attention to the external circumstances of the theatre. The reason lies in the empirical character of the American stage. With few exceptions, the classic theatre of the Continent is primarily literary: the stage history of a play does not normally influence its text. The American play, on the other hand, usually is not printed until it has been successfully produced. Producers, directors, actors, and even the audiences help to create the final versions. The changes that make a play usable for the stage are incorporated into the text. The American drama could almost be called a by-product of the stage. Hence the curious—at times perhaps even healthy—fusion of practical with literary matters.

Unfortunately perhaps, not all important American playwrights have used the essay to express themselves; nevertheless, this collection of nondramatic writing by our playwrights reflects the interesting paradox of the theatre of the United States: a continent larger than Europe is represented mainly by the theatre of one city—New York —but the audiences supporting this theatre are as mixed and varied as New York's population itself. Moreover, audiences are perpetually renewed and supplemented by Americans from all parts of the country. Thus, one may say that, while the American theatre suffers from a provincialism of the East Coast in respect to stage presentations, it is unlimited in the wealth of its subject matter. The essays in this collection attempt to cope with almost every complex question that could be raised in connection with the drama and theatre of the United States. If nothing else, all of them tell us a great deal about the author as a playwright and a human being. All of them show deep concern with the life of the drama.

American Playwrights
on Drama

EUGENE O'NEILL

Strindberg and Our Theatre

IN CREATING a modern theatre which we hope will liberate for significant expression a fresh elation and joy in experimental production, it is the most apt symbol of our good intentions that we start with a play by August Strindberg; for Strindberg was the precursor of all modernity in our present theatre just as Ibsen, a lesser man as he himself surmised, was the father of the modernity of twenty years or so ago when it was believed that *A Doll's House* wasn't— just that.

Strindberg still remains among the most modern of moderns, the greatest interpreter in the theatre of the characteristic spiritual conflicts which constitute the drama —the blood!—of our lives today. He carried naturalism to a logical attainment of such poignant intensity that, if the work of any other playwright is to be called "naturalism," we must classify a play like *The Dance of Death* as "supernaturalism" and place it in a class by itself, exclusively Strindberg's since no one before or after him has had the genius to qualify.

Yet it is only by means of some form of "super-naturalism" that we may express in the theatre what we comprehend intuitively of that self-defeating self-obsession which is the discount we moderns have to pay for the loan of life. The old "naturalism"—or "realism," if you prefer (would to God some genius were gigantic enough to define clearly the separateness of these terms once and for all)—no longer applies. It represents our fathers' daring aspirations

Reprinted with the permission of Carlotta Monterey O'Neill. First published in Provincetown Playbill, no. 1, season 1923-24.

toward self-recognition by holding the family Kodak up to ill-nature. But to us their old audacity is blague; we have taken too many snapshots of each other in every graceless position; we have endured too much from the banality of surfaces. We are ashamed of having peeked through so many keyholes, squinting always at heavy, uninspired bodies—the fat facts—with not a nude spirit among them; we have been sick with appearances and are convalescing; we "wipe out and pass on" to some as yet unrealized region where our souls, maddened by loneliness and the ignoble inarticulateness of flesh, are slowly evolving their new language of kinship.

Strindberg knew and suffered with our struggle years before many of us were born. He expressed it by intensifying the method of his time and by foreshadowing both in content and form the methods to come. All that is enduring in what we loosely call "Expressionism"—all that is artistically valid and sound theatre—can be clearly traced back through Wedekind to Strindberg's *The Dream Play, There Are Crimes and Crimes, The Spook Sonata,* etc.

Hence, *The Spook Sonata* at our Playhouse. One of the most difficult of Strindberg's "behind-life" (if I may coin the term) plays to interpret with insight and distinction—but the difficult is properly our special task, or we have no good reason for existing. Truth, in the theatre as in life, is eternally difficult, just as the easy is the everlasting lie.

So pray with us—and (although we don't need it, of course, but it may do us some good) for us.

EUGENE O'NEILL

Working Notes and Extracts from a Fragmentary Work Diary

1. (*Spring—1926*)

Modern psychological drama using one of the old legend plots of Greek tragedy for its basic theme—the Electra story?—the Medea? Is it possible to get modern psychological approximation of Greek sense of fate into such a play, which an intelligent audience of today, possessed of no belief in gods or supernatural retribution, could accept and be moved by?—

2. (*October, 1928—Arabian Sea en route for China*)

Greek tragedy plot idea—story of Electra and family psychologically most interesting—most comprehensive intense basic human interrelationships—can be easily widened in scope to include still others.

3. (*November, 1928—China Sea*)

Greek plot idea—give modern Electra figure in play tragic ending worthy of character. In Greek story she peters out into undramatic married banality. Such a character contained too much tragic fate within her soul to permit this —why should Furies have let Electra escape unpunished? Why did the chain of fated crime and retribution ignore her mother's murderess?—a weakness in what remains to

Reprinted with the permission of Carlotta Monterey O'Neill. First published as "O'Neill's Own Story of *Electra* in the Making" in New York *Herald-Tribune* of November 3, 1931. A photostat of the original manuscript was attached to the 1931 "Special Edition" of *Mourning Becomes Electra* published by Horace Liveright, Inc.

us of Greek tragedy that there is no play about Electra's life after the murder of Clytemnestra. Surely it possesses as imaginative tragic possibilities as any of their plots!

4. (*Cap d'Ail, France—April, 1929*)

Greek tragedy plot idea—No matter in what period of American history play is laid, must remain a modern psychological drama—nothing to do with period except to use it as a mask—What war?—Revolution too far off and too clogged in people's minds with romantic grammar-school-history associations. World War too near and recognizable in its obstructing (for my purpose) minor aspects and superficial character identifications (audience would not see fated wood because too busy recalling trees)—needs distance and perspective—period not too distant for audience to associate itself with, yet possessing costume, etc.—possessing sufficient mask of time and space, so that audiences will unconsciously grasp at once, it is primarily drama of hidden life forces—fate—behind lives of characters. Civil War is only possibility—fits into picture—Civil War as background for drama of murderous family love and hate—

5. (*Cap d'Ail, France—April, 1929*)

(Greek plot idea)—Lay in New England small seaport, shipbuilding town—family town's best—shipbuilders and owners—wealthy for period—Agamemnon character town's leading citizen, Mayor before war, now Brigadier General Grant's Army—opening act of play day of Lee's surrender —house Greek temple front type that was rage in 1st half 19th century—(this fits in well and absolutely justifiable, not forced Greek similarity)—This home of New England House of Atreus was built in 1830, say, by Atreus character, Agamemnon's father—grotesque perversion of everything Greek temple expressed of meaning of life—(New England background best possible dramatically for Greek plot of crime and retribution, chain of fate—Puritan conviction of man born to sin and punishment—Orestes' furies within him, his conscience—etc.)

Departures from Greek story—Electra loves Aegisthus —always fated to be mother's rival in love, always defeated—first for father's love, then for brother's, finally for Aegisthus'—reason for Clytemnestra's hatred for Agamemnon sexual frustration by his puritan sense of guilt turning love to lust (she had romantic love for him before marriage)—omit Iphigenia and Chrysothemis from children—only Orestes and Electra—no Cassandra—keep exact family relationship of Aegisthus (first cousin Agamemnon)—keep general outline of rivalry, hatred, love, lust, revenge in past between Agamemnon's father, Atreus, and Aegisthus' father, Thyestes (in legend Thyestes seduces Aërope, wife of Atreus)—hatred of Atreus for brother—revenge—banishment—(keep general spirit of this but pay no attention to details of legend) Clytemnestra persuades Aegisthus against his will to help her murder Agamemnon (my Aegisthus character weaker, more human, and less evil character, has conscience of sort)—method of murder, poison (woman's weapon)—Aegisthus bears strong facial resemblance to Agamemnon and Orestes—his resemblance to Orestes attracts Clytemnestra—his resemblance to her father attracts Electra—Electra adores father, devoted to brother (who resembles father), hates mother—Orestes adores mother, devoted to sister (whose face resembles mother's) so hates his father—Agamemnon, frustrated in love for Clytemnestra, adores daughter, Electra, who resembles her, hates and is jealous of his son, Orestes—etc.—work out this symbol of family resemblances and identification (as visible sign of the family fate) still further—use masks (?)

6. (*Cap d'Ail, France—May, 1929*)

(Greek plot idea)—Names of characters—use characteristic names with some similarity to Greek ones—for main characters, at least—but don't strain after this and make it a stunt—no real importance, only convenience in picking—right names always tough job.

Agamemnon—(Asa), (Ezra) Mannon
Clytemnestra—Christine (?)
Orestes—Orin

{
Electra—Eleanor (?) Ellen (?) Elsa (?)
Laodicea—Lavinia (this sounds more like it) Vinnie (Called in family)
}

Aegisthus—Augustus (?) Alan Adam (?)
Pylades—Paul (?) Peter (?)
Hermione—Hazel—Hesther

7. (*Cap d'Ail, France—May, 1929*)

(Greek plot idea)—Title—*Mourning Becomes Electra*—
that is, in old sense of word—it befits—it becomes Electra
to mourn—it is her fate,—also, in usual sense (made ironi-
cal here), mourning (black) is becoming to her—it is the
only color that becomes her destiny—

8. (*Cap d'Ail, France—May, 1929*)

Mourning Becomes Electra—No chance getting full value
material into one play or even two—must follow Greek
practice and make it trilogy—first play Agamemnon's
home-coming and murder—second, Electra's revenge on
mother and lover, using Orestes to help her—third play,
retribution Orestes and Electra.

Give each play a separate title—*Mourning Becomes
Electra* title for trilogy as whole—first play, *Home-coming*
—second, (?)—third, *The Haunted.*

9. (*Cap d'Ail, France—May, 1929*)

Mourning Becomes Electra—Technique—for first draft
use comparatively straight realism—this first draft only
for purpose of plot material into definite form—then lay
aside for period and later decide how to go to final version—what departures necessary—whether to use masks,
soliloquies, asides, etc.—

**10. (*Le Plessis, St. Antoine-du-Rocher, France—
     June 20, 1929*)**

Mourning Becomes Electra—Finished scenario first play,
Home-coming.

**11. (*Le Plessis, St. Antoine-du-Rocher, France—
     July 11, 1929*)**

Mourning Becomes Electra—Finished scenario second play,
The Hunted—what an advantage it was (from a plotter's
standpoint, at least) for authors in other times who wrote
about kings—could commit murder without having to

dodge detection, arrest, trial scenes for their characters—
I have to waste a lot of ingenuity to enable my plotters to
get away with it without suspicion!—still, even history of
comparatively recent crimes (where they happen among
people supposedly respectable) shows that rural authorities
easily hoodwinked—the poisoning of Mannon in *Home-coming* would probably never be suspected (under the
same circumstances) even in New England town of today,
let alone in 1865.

12. (*Le Plessis, St. Antoine-du-Rocher, France—
     August, 1929*)

Mourning Becomes Electra—Finished scenario third play,
The Haunted—have given my Yankee Electra tragic end
worthy of her—and Orestes, too.

13. (*Le Plessis, St. Antoine-du-Rocher, France—
     Sept., 1929*)

Started writing 1st draft—*Mourning Becomes Electra*.

14. (*Le Plessis, St. Antoine-du-Rocher, France—
     Oct., 1929*)

After several false starts, all rotten, think I have hit right
line for first draft now.

15. (*Le Plessis, St. Antoine-du-Rocher, France—
     Feb. 21, 1930*)

Finished 1st draft *M. B. E.*—lay aside now for at least
month—

16. (*Le Plessis, St. Antoine-du-Rocher, France—
     March 27, 1930*)

Read over first draft *M. B. E.*—scrawny stuff but serves
purpose as first draft—parts damned thrilling but lots more
lousy—not enough meat—don't like Aegisthus' character—
hackneyed and thin—must find new one—not enough of
sense of fate hovering over characters, fate of family—
living in the house built by Atreus' hatred (Abe Mannon)
—a psychological fate—reading this first draft I get feeling
that more of my idea was left out of play than there is in
it!—In next version I must correct this at all costs—run

the risk of going to other cluttered-up extreme—use every means to gain added depth and scope—can always cut what is unnecessary afterwards—will write second draft using half masks and an *Interlude* technique (combination *Lazarus* and *Interlude*) and see what can be gotten out of that—think these will aid me to get just the right effect—must get more distance and perspective—more sense of fate—more sense of the unreal behind what we call reality which is the real reality!—The unrealistic truth wearing the mask of lying reality, that is the right feeling for this trilogy, if I can only catch it! Stick to modern tempo of dialogue without attempt at pretence of Civil Wartime lingo. That part of 1st draft is right. Obtain more fixed formal structure for first play which succeeding plays will reiterate—pattern of exterior and interior scenes, beginning and ending with exterior in each play—with the one ship scene at the center of the second play (this, center of whole work) emphasizing sea background of family and symbolic motive of sea as means of escape and release—use townsfolk at the beginning of each play, outside house, as fixed chorus pattern—representing prying, commenting, curious town as an ever-present background for the drama of the Mannon family. Develop South Sea Island motive—its appeal for them all (in various aspects)—release, peace, security, beauty, freedom of conscience, sinlessness, etc.—longing for the primitive—and mother symbol—yearning for prenatal non-competitive freedom from fear—make this Island theme recurrent motive—Characterization—Exclude as far as possible and consistent with living people, the easy superficial characterization of individual mannerisms—unless these mannerisms are inevitable fingerprints of inner nature—essential revelations. This applies to main people of trilogy. Townsfolk, on the other hand, should be confined to exterior characterization—main characters too interior—Peter and Hazel should be almost characterless, judged from either of these angles—they are the untroubled, contented "good," a sweet, constant unselfconscious, untempted virtue amid which evil passion works, unrecognized by them—(until end)—but emphasized by their contrast. Resemblance of characters by use of masks intensify Mannon family resemblance between Ezra and

Orin and Adam (and family portraits), and between Christine and Lavinia—peculiar gold-brown hair exactly alike in Lavinia and her mother—same as hair of the dead woman, Adam's mother, whom Ezra's father and uncle had loved—who started the chain of recurrent love and hatred and revenge—emphasize this motivating fate out of past—hair of women another recurrent motive—strange, hidden psychic identity of Christine with the dead woman and of Lavinia (in spite of her father—Mannon imitative mannerisms) with her mother—and of Adam with the Mannons he hates, as well as of Orin with his father— The chanty "Shenandoah"—use this more—as a sort of theme song—its simple sad rhythm of hopeless sea longing peculiarly significant—even the stupid words have striking meaning when considered in relation to tragic events in play—In my scrawny first draft bare melodrama of plot runs away with my intent—this must be corrected in second draft—the unavoidable entire melodramatic action must be felt as working out of psychic fate from past— thereby attain tragic significance—or else!—a hell of a problem, a modern tragic interpretation of classic fate without benefit of gods—for it must, before everything remain modern psychological play—fate springing out of the family—

17. (*Le Plessis—March 31, 1930*)
Start writing 2nd draft.

18. (*Le Plessis—July 11, 1930*)
Finish 2nd draft—feel drained out—have been working morning, afternoon and night every day, without a single let-up—never worked so intensively over such a long period as I have on this damn' trilogy—wish now I'd never attempted the damn' thing—bitten off more than can chew?—Too close to it to see anything but blur of words—discouraged reaction natural now—after all, do know I was deeply moved by each play as I wrote it—that test has always proved valid heretofore—lay it aside now —we are off to Paris tomorrow—nice little vacation in dentist's chair scheduled! Best anodyne for pernicious brooding over one's inadequacies, that!—anything else

seems like the best of all possible when your nerves are prancing to sweet and low down of a dental drill!—

19. (*Le Plessis*—*July 18, 1930*)

Read the trilogy—much better than I feared—but needs a lot more work before it will be anything like right—chief thing, thought asides now seem entirely unnecessary—don't reveal anything about the characters I can't bring out quite naturally in their talk or their soliloquies when alone—simply get in the way of the play's drive, make the line waver, cause action to halt and limp—must be deleted in toto—Warning!—always hereafter regard with suspicion hangover inclination to use "Interlude" technique regardless—that was what principally hurt "Dynamo," being forced into thought-asides method which was quite alien to essential psychological form of its characters—did not ring true—only clogged up play arbitrarily with obvious author's mannerisms—saw this when I re-read it after return from East—too late! "Interlude" aside technique is special expression for special type of modern neurotic, disintegrated soul—when dealing with simple direct folk or characters of strong will and intense passions, it is superfluous show-shop "business."

20. (*Le Plessis*—*July 19, 1930*)

Read trilogy again—don't like the soliloquies in their present disjointed thought-prose formula—and my use of half masks on the main protagonists seems to obscure meaning of resemblance between characters instead of dramatically intensifying this meaning—masks introduce other connotations not wanted [in] these plays—have strong feeling there should be much more definite interrelationship between characters' masks and soliloquies, that soliloquies should be arbitrarily set in a stylized form that will be the exact expression of stylized mask symbol—Rewrite all soliloquies in plays along this line—introduce new ones so that soliloquies will recur in a fixed pattern throughout, fitting into structural pattern repeated in each play—try for prose with simple forceful repeating accent and rhythm which will express driving insistent compulsion of passions engendered in family past, which constitute family fate (always remembering fate from within the family is modern psychological approximation of the Greek conception of fate from without, from the supernatural).

21. (*Le Plessis—July 20, 1930*)

Start rewriting, cutting out all asides, stylizing soliloquies as per new conception—think I have hit on right rhythm of prose—monotonous, simple words driving insistence—tom tom from "Jones" in thought repetition—

22. (*Le Plessis—Sept. 16, 1930*)

Finished rewriting—lay aside for a while—one thing am certain of right now, omitting asides has helped plays enormously—

23. (*Paris—Sept. 20, 1930*)

Read and carefully reread this last stylized-soliloquies version—absolutely convinced they don't do!—feel as I felt about asides in version before this, that they held up plays, break rhythm, clog flow of dramatic development, reveal nothing of characters' motives, secret desires or dreams, that can't be shown directly or clearly suggested in their pantomine or talk—some of these soliloquies are gratifying as pieces of writing in themselves (most of them are not!) but even then they don't belong—have no inherent place in structure—they must come out—and with them the half-masks of the Mannons must go too—obtrude themselves too much into the foreground—introduce an obvious duality-of-character symbolism quite outside my intent in these plays—and if I leave out soliloquies, there is no excuse for these half-masks anyway—save for some future play.

24. (*Paris—Sept. 21, 1930*)

Scheme for revision and final version—in spite of labor on this stylized conception am glad I did it—time not wasted —learned a lot—stylized solil. uncovered new insights into characters and recurrent themes—job now is to get all this in naturally in straight dialogue—as simple and direct and dynamic as possible—with as few words—stop doing things to these characters—let them reveal themselves—

in spite of (or because of!) their long locked-up passions, I feel them burning to do just this!

Keep mask conception—but as Mannon *background*, not foreground!—what I want from this mask concept is a dramatic arresting visual symbol of the separateness, the fated isolation of this family, the mark of their fate which makes them dramatically distinct from rest of world—I see now how to retain this effect without the use of built masks—by make-up—in *repose* (that is, *background*) the Mannon faces are like life-like death masks—(death-in-life motive, return to death-with-peace yearning that runs through plays)—this can be gotten very effectively by make-up, as can also the family resemblance—(make-up isn't a lost art in European theatre, why should it be in ours?—only our shiftless inefficiency)—I can visualize the death-mask-like expression of characters' faces in repose suddenly being torn open by passion as extraordinarily effective—moreover, its exact visual representation of what I want expressed—Rewrite trilogy along these lines—and get more architectural fixed form into outer structure—and more composition (in musical sense) into inner structure—more definite recurrence of themes ("Island" death fear and death wish, the family past, etc.)—always bearing in mind—Mannon drama takes place on a plane where outer reality is mask of true fated reality—unreal realism—

Make into even more definite fixed pattern superficial characteristic type realism of the chorus of the town (the world outside which always sees without really seeing or understanding) and the simple healthy normality—goodness—of Hazel and Peter.

Repetition of the same scene—in its essential spirit, sometimes even in its exact words, but between different characters—following plays as development of fate—theme demands this repetition—Mannon & Christine (about Brant) in 1st play, Christine & Orin (about Brant) in second play—Mannon & Christine in 4th act, 1st play, Lavinia & Orin in 2nd act, 3rd play—etc.

25. (*Le Plessis—Sept. 23, 1930*)

Start rewriting.

26. (*Le Plessis—Oct. 15, 1930*)

Finish rewriting—off for trip to Spain and Morocco.

27. (*Le Plessis—Nov. 19, 1930*)

Read last version—fairly well satisfied—got right line to it, at least—and quality I want—but needs considerable work yet—several new ideas I want to try out—may bring added value—not sure—only way try and see—start on this at once.

28. (*Paris—Jan. 10, 1931*)

Have finished most of new stuff—getting plays typed as I work—

29. (*Paris—Feb. 2, 1931*)

Typing finished with all new stuff in—let it rest now—

30. (*Le Plessis—Feb. 7, 1931*)

Read over—don't like most of new stuff—all right but introduces too many added complications—trying to get added values has blurred those I had—too much of muchness—would need another play added to do it right—and would be wrong even then!—can't crowd intuitions all hidden aspects of life form into one work!—I better throw most of this new stuff out—some valuable and can be condensed and retained—but in general revert entirely to former version.

31. (*Le Plessis—Feb. 20, 1931*)

Revision finished—off to Canary Islands for a sun and sea vacation—

32. (*Las Palmas—Canary Islands—March 8, 1931*)

Read typed script—looks damned good to me—funny how typed pages bring out clearly values that too-long familiarity with longhand had rendered vague and undynamic—but plenty of work to do—no vacation here—script much too long, of course—needs cutting and condensing throughout—must rewrite end of *The Hunted*—weak now—Christine's talk to Lavinia toward end bad stuff—first scene of

Act One *The Haunted* also needs rewriting and pointing
up—flabby and faltering as now written—ends of Scenes
One & Two *The Hunted* also need work—

33. (*Las Palmas—March 26, 1931*)

Finished work—return to France (Marseilles) Casablanca
and Tangier tomorrow—script retyped—

34. (*Paris—April 4, 1931*)

Decide change Scenes One & Two, Act One, *The Hunted*
to Acts One & Two—they are properly acts, not scenes—
but Scene One Act One of *The Haunted* is properly a scene
—question of feeling, this!—no rules about it—

35. (*Paris—April 9, 1931*)

New script retyped—copies off to Guild—

36. (*Northport—August, 1931*)

Read over galley proofs from Liveright—after nearly four
months of not looking at this trilogy, get fairly fresh impact—moved by it—has power and drive and the strange
quality of unreal reality I wanted—main purpose seems to
me soundly achieved—there is a feeling of fate in it, or I
am a fool—a psychological modern approximation of the
fate in the Greek tragedies on this theme—attained without benefit of supernatural—

And technically (although this is of minor importance,
naturally) I flatter myself it is unique thing in dramaturgy
—each play complete episode completely realized but at
same time, which is the important point, not complete in
that its end begins following play and demands that play
as an inevitable sequel—few trilogies in existence in drama
of all time and none of them has this quality which, in
any time under any conditions, could not have failed to
prove an asset—if gained without harm to the separate
play, of course, as I believe I have done.

(*Interlude* never got credit for this technical virtue—
without which its successful production would have been
impossible—that the first part rounded out a complete section of Nina's life with a definite beginning and end and
yet contained the suspense at its end which called for Part

Two—otherwise dinner interval would have wrecked it—no other two-part play, as far as I know, has accomplished this synthesis of end and beginning—)

37. (*Northport—August, 1931*)

Work on galley proofs—cutting is needed, especially in first and third plays—

38. (*Northport—Sept., 1931*)

Work on second galleys—several points strike me—work I did at Canary Islands was of great value in most of results—but feel now a few things eliminated there should be restored—Lavinia's last appeal to Peter near very end—some things in Act Two which help to clear it up—this Act Two of *The Haunted* is weak spot still—needs rearranging—but will postpone final decision on this until I hear cast read plays—then it will hit my ear.

MAXWELL ANDERSON

Poetry in the Theatre

EXPERIMENT in the theatre is made difficult and expensive by the fact that a play must find an audience at once or have no chance of finding one later. There is no instance in the theatre of a writer who left behind him a body of unappreciated work which slowly found its public, as, for example, the work of Shelley and Keats found a belated public after they had left the scene. It follows that the playwright must pluck from the air about him a fable which will be of immediate interest to his time and hour, and relate it in a fashion acceptable to his neighbors. That is the job for which he is paid. But he will also try to make that fable coincide with something in himself that he wants to put in words. A certain cleverness in striking a compromise between the world about him and the world within has characterized the work of the greatest as well as the least of successful playwrights, for they must all take an audience with them if they are to continue to function. Some may consider it blasphemy to state that this compromise must be a considered and conscious act—will believe that the writer should look in his heart and write—but in the theatre such an attitude leaves the achievement entirely to chance, and a purely chance achievement is not an artistic one.

Yet when a writer sits down before white paper to make

this necessary compromise he finds himself alone among imponderables. Nobody has ever known definitely what any audience wanted. A choice must be made with only intuition and a mass of usually irrelevant information as the guides. One who thinks more of his job than his fame will therefore play safe by repressing his personal preferences and going all the way in the direction of what he believes the public wants. One who thinks as much of his fame as of his job will often hope the public is ready for a theme only because he wishes to treat it—or ready for a dramatic method only because he wishes to employ it.

I may have been somewhat guilty of this last misapprehension in *Winterset*, for I have a strong and chronic hope that the theatre of this country will outgrow the phase of journalistic social comment and reach occasionally into the upper air of poetic tragedy. I believe with Goethe that dramatic poetry is man's greatest achievement on his earth so far, and I believe with the early Bernard Shaw that the theatre is essentially a cathedral of the spirit, devoted to the exaltation of men, and boasting an apostolic succession of inspired high priests which extends further into the past than the Christian line founded by Saint Peter. It has been, even at its best, a democratic temple, decorated with more gargoyles than saints, generously open to wits, clowns, excoriating satirists, false prophets, and crowds of moneychangers with a heavy investment in the mysteries. Lately it has recognized the mysteries only as a side show, and has been overrun with guides who prove to an eager public that all saints are plaster and all prophets fakes.

When Shaw began his furious critical assault on the romantic theatre which was lingering out the last decade of the nineteenth century, he became the prophet of the theatre of realistic social protest which he has dominated in England during his lifetime and which is still the controlling pattern for plays of the English-speaking stage. A few original and outstanding playwrights, J. M. Synge, Sean O'Casey, and Eugene O'Neill among them, may seem to fall completely outside the Shavian category. Synge was too poetic, symbolic, and savage to work in any social harness, O'Casey's world-searing irony is too tremendous to come under the head of protest, and O'Neill has been

seeking an escape from realism throughout his whole career.
All three went beyond Shaw's amusing balance and clarity
into a tragic, sinister, and often brutal world. Synge wrote
of that world with extraordinary beauty and a lethal precision; O'Casey and O'Neill write of it with passion and a
sometimes choking defiance. O'Casey, in addition, has a
power over words which lifts such a play as *The Plough
and the Stars* out of its local setting and makes it, in my
opinion, the finest contemporary play I have seen in the
theatre.

But none of these three, nor Shaw himself, has written
plays which we can set unquestioningly beside the best we
can pick up in the library—and the reason for that is a
fairly simple one. Our modern dramatists (with the exception of O'Casey, who has lately tried his 'prentice wings)
are not poets, and the best prose in the world is inferior on
the stage to the best poetry. It is the fashion, I know, to
say that poetry is a matter of content and emotion, not of
form, but this is said in an age of prose by prose writers
who have not studied the effect of form on content or who
wish to believe there is no limit to the scope of the form
they have mastered. To me it is inescapable that prose is
the language of information and poetry the language of
emotion. Prose can be stretched to carry emotion, and in
some exceptional cases, as in Synge's and O'Casey's plays,
can occasionally rise to poetic heights by substituting the
unfamiliar speech rhythms of an untutored people for the
rhythm of verse. But under the strain of an emotion the
ordinary prose of our stage breaks down into inarticulateness, just as it does in life. Hence the cult of understatement, hence the realistic drama in which the climax is
reached in an eloquent gesture or a moment of meaningful
silence.

The majority of present-day playgoers have never seen
any other kind of play and see no reason why there should
be any other. So emphatic is this feeling that one is doubt-
ful of being able to explain to this majority that verse was
once the accepted convention on the stage, as prose is now,
that prose fought its way into the playbooks with difficulty
at the beginning of the scientific era in which we live and
will hold its place there only so long as men make a re-

ligion of fact and believe that information, conveyed in statistical language, can make them free.

For the stage is still a cathedral, but just now a journalistic one, dominated by those who wish to offer something immediate about our political, social, or economic life. Like every other existing condition it gives the illusion of permanence, but it will change. An age of reason will be followed once more by an age of faith in things unseen. The cathedral will then house the mysteries again, along with the jugglers and the vendors of rose-colored spectacles. What faith men will then have, when they have lost their certainty of salvation through laboratory work, I don't know, having myself only a faith that men will have a faith. But that it will involve a desire for poetry after our starvation diet of prose I have no doubt. Men have not been altered by the invention of airplanes and the radio. They are still alone and frightened, holding their chance tenure of life in utter isolation in this desolate region of revolving fires. Science may answer a few necessary questions for them, but in the end science itself is obliged to say that the fact is created by the spirit, not spirit by the fact. Our leading scientists are already coming to this conclusion, rather reluctantly and with some surprise.

Unless I am greatly mistaken, many members of the theatre audience have anticipated this conclusion by one of those intuitional short-cuts which confound the devotees of pure reason, and are not only ready but impatient for plays which will take up again the consideration of man's place and destiny in prophetic rather than prosaic terms. It is incumbent on the dramatist to be a poet, and incumbent on the poet to be prophet, dreamer, and interpreter of the racial dream. Men have come a long way from the salt water in the millions of years that lie behind them, and have a long way to go in the millions of years that lie ahead. We shall not always be as we are—but what we are to become depends on what we dream and desire. The theatre, more than any other art, has the power to weld and determine what the race dreams into what the race will become. All this may sound rather farfetched in the face of our present Broadway, and Broadway may laugh at it unconscionably, but Broadway is itself as transient as the

real-estate values under its feet. Those of us who fail to
outlive the street in which we work will fail because we
have accepted its valuations and measured our product by
them.

For though on the surface we are still a pioneer people,
ashamed of aspiration, offended by the deliberate quest for
beauty, able to accept beauty only when it seems achieved
by accident, our pioneer days are over and we must set
about molding ourselves at least one art form worthy of
the leading nation of the world or be set down finally as
barbarians and carry that name with us into the darkness
to which all nations sooner or later descend. Our theatre is
the one really living American art. It has size, vitality, and
popular interest. But it is still in the awkward and self-
conscious age, concealing its dreams by clowning, bur-
lesquing the things it most admires. Those who have read
their literary history carefully know that now is the time
for our native amusements to be transformed into a national art of power and beauty. It needs the touch of a
great poet to make the transformation, a poet comparable
to Aeschylus in Greece or Marlowe in England. Without at
least one such we shall never have a great theatre in this
country, and he must come soon, for these chances don't
endure forever.

I must add, lest I be misunderstood, that I have not
mistaken myself for this impending phenomenon. I have
made my living as teacher, journalist, and playwright and
have only that skill as a poet which may come from long
practice of an art I have loved and studied and cannot let
alone. When I wrote my first play, *White Desert,* I wrote
it in verse because I was weary of plays in prose that never
lifted from the ground. It failed, and I did not come back
to verse again until I had discovered that poetic tragedy
had never been successfully written about its own place and
time. There is not one tragedy by Aeschylus, Sophocles,
Euripides, Shakespeare, Corneille, or Racine which did not
have the advantage of a setting either far away or long
ago. With this admonition in mind I wrote *Elizabeth the
Queen* and a succession of historical plays in verse, some
of them successful, and found myself immediately labeled
a historical and romantic playwright, two terms I found

equally distasteful. *Winterset* is largely in verse, and treats a contemporary tragic theme, which makes it more of an experiment than I could wish, for the great masters themselves never tried to make tragic poetry out of the stuff of their own times. To do so is to attempt to establish a new convention, one that may prove impossible of acceptance, but to which I was driven by the lively historical sense of our day—a knowledge of period, costume, and manners which almost shuts off the writer on historical themes from contemporary comment. Whether or not I have solved the problem in *Winterset* is probably of little moment. But it must be solved if we are to have a great theatre in America. Our theatre has not yet produced anything worthy to endure—and endurance, though it may be a fallible test, is the only test of excellence.

JOHN HOWARD LAWSON

The Social Framework

LET US assume that the suicide of a faithful wife takes place under conditions which are dramatically ideal—the situation suggests intense possibilities of pity and terror; the social implications are far-reaching. But the system of causation which leads to this event is still untouched; we are dealing *only* with possibilities and implications, because the effect of the event cannot be understood until its causes are dramatized.

The playwright *knows* the meaning of the situation; the potential pity and terror are real to him. But he must prove that his conception of reality is justified; he must show the whole scheme of things which made this event true in the deepest sense.

The playwright is faced by an infinite multiplicity of possible causes. He might very possibly begin by listing a number of questions in connection with the history of the event. Perhaps the most superficial fact is the fact that the husband has fallen in love with another woman. Many women do not kill themselves on this account. We cannot analyze the psychological factors in the case without discovering that far-reaching social and economic problems must be investigated. It is evident that the wife's relationship to her husband is of a special emotional character. This means that her relationship to her environment is also of a special character. We must make a study of the en-

Reprinted by permission of G. P. Putnam's Sons from *Theory and Technique of Playwriting* by John Howard Lawson. Copyright © 1964 by John Howard Lawson. This is a somewhat shortened version of the chapter on "The Social Framework." The book was published originally in 1936.

vironment, her emotional attitudes toward other persons, her heredity, education, and economic status. This in turn forces us to consider the heredity, education, and economic status of all the people with whom she is associated. Do they earn their money, or live on income? What has been the amount of their income during the past ten years, where does it come from, and how do they spend it? What are their amusements, their cultural experiences? What are their ethical standards and how far do they adhere to these in practice? What is their attitude toward marriage and what events have conditioned this attitude? What has been their sexual experience? Have they any children? If not, why not?

These factors can be traced back through many years. But the woman's personal history, psychologically and physically, is also of great interest: what has been the state of her health? Has she shown any neurotic symptoms? We want to know whether she has shown any previous disposition toward suicide: when, and under what conditions? We want to know about her girlhood, her physical and mental activities as a child.

It may seem necessary to construct a similar personal history of several of the other characters—particularly of the husband and of the other woman. Each personal investigation leads us into a new complex of relationships, involving differences in social and psychological determinants.

This list seems forbidding, but it is only a hasty suggestion of the possible lines of speculation which are open to the dramatist in organizing his material. Aside from its incompleteness, what impression does this list convey? The questions are not very specific, and tend to be psychological rather than factual, static rather than dynamic. But it is precisely objective, factual, dynamic events for which we are searching. The field covered by these questions must be covered—but it cannot be covered *in this way*. The attempt to construct a complete history of everything which led to the moment of climax would lead to the accumulation of a vast amount of unmanageable data. If carried out uncompromisingly, such an undertaking would be more ambitious than the whole lifework of Proust.

The process of selection is not *a narrative process*. The

playwright is not looking for illustrative or psychological material, but for a system of actions; just as the final climax sums up a maximum change of equilibrium between individuals and their environment, each of the subordinate crises is a change of equilibrium leading to the maximum change. Each crisis is effective in proportion to its compression and extension. No action of the play can be more significant than the root-action, because in that case it would go beyond the scope of the play.

A more or less narrative list such as the one outlined is only useful as a means of suggesting the sort of events for which we are searching—events which compress the emotional lives of the characters in moments of explosive tension, and which extend as far as possible in their effect on the environment.

In planning the wider framework of the play, the dramatist is organizing material which is obviously less dramatic than the play itself. Events which are assumed to have happened before the opening of the drama, or which are reported during the action, or which take place off-stage or between the acts, cannot be as vital as the visible action behind the footlights. But it must not be supposed that the outer framework is a shadowy fiction, covered by a few vague references to the past lives of the characters and the social forces of the period. Since the larger pattern of events represents the scope of the playwright's conception, it must be dramatized as fully as possible. The playwright who thinks of the ultimate causes underlying his drama in narrative terms will carry over some of this narrative form into the stage-action. By visualizing these ultimate causes in meaningful and cumulative crises, the playwright establishes the basis for the later and more detailed selection of the stage-action. The reserve of events, behind and around the play, gives sweep and sureness to the action, and gives more meaning to every line of dialogue, every gesture, every situation.

We now have two principles which give us additional guidance in studying the preconditions leading to a climactic situation: (1) we are looking only for crises; (2) we are seeking to outline a system of events which not only covers the inner action of the play, but which extends the concept of social necessity (the whole scheme of life in which the climax is placed) to the limit of its possibilities. We find that some of these events show a much greater explosiveness of conscious will than others: these are the most dynamic events, those which cause the most serious changes in the environment and which have the greatest driving force. But these explosive moments are produced by other events, which are less explosive because they involve a more impregnable social necessity opposed to a less awakened conscious will. What is this more impregnable social necessity and where does it come from? It comes from still earlier explosions of conscious will which have been sufficiently powerful to change and crystallize conditions in this fixed form: it is this form of apparently impregnable social necessity which defines the limits of the dramatic scheme. The playwright accepts this necessity as the picture of reality in which the play is framed. He cannot go *beyond* this necessity and investigate the acts of will which created it, because to do so would be to question its ultimate value and to deny the concept of reality as it is embodied in his climax.

The less explosive events are those which constitute the outer framework: these events are dramatic and include the exercise of conscious will; but they are less dynamic; they have less effect on the environment; they show the solidity of the social forces which mold the conscious wills of the characters and which are the ultimate obstacles which the conscious wills must face.

If we return to the list of questions concerning the wife's suicide, and attempt to apply these principles, we find that we must arrange the questions in groups and attempt to create a situation which is the culmination of the social and psychological factors involved. For example: What is the economic status of the family? What has been the amount of their income during the past ten years, where does it come from, and how do they spend it? We are not interested in statistics, although statistics may be of value in dramatizing the issue; but we must find an event which has the broadest possible implications; the event need not be a financial crisis; we are interested in the way in which money affects the conscious wills of these people, how it determines

their relationship to people of their own class and those of
other classes, how it colors their prejudices, illusions, modes
of thought. The root-action serves as our reference point:
the event must therefore embody the elements of the root-
action: the woman's attitude toward suicide or her fear of
death, her sentimental attitude toward marriage and love,
her emotional dependence and lack of self-confidence. An
economic situation will serve to expose the social roots of
these attitudes.

The same principle applies in analyzing the childhood of
our leading character. We do not wish to find isolated or
sensational events which have some psychological connection with the climax; such a connection, isolated from the
background, would probably be static rather than dynamic.
A woman's childhood is not a set of major and minor incidents to be catalogued, but a process to be considered as a
whole. The key to this process is the fact that she ended
her life under certain known conditions. We assume that
the sum-total of this childhood is revealed in a basic conflict between the child and its environment (in which other
persons play a part); we must consider both the other persons and the environment as a whole. We know the final
stage of the conflict. We want to crystallize the earlier stages
in climactic events.

If the background of the play is English middle-class
country life, we must consider the profound changes which
have taken place in this life: the heartbreak houses of the
gentry shaken by the European war; the armistice celebrated
by people drunk with weariness and hope; the breaking
down of old social values; the profound economic disturb-
ances.

The plays of Ibsen show a remarkably thorough dramatization of the outer framework. Events which happened in
the past, in the childhood of the characters, play a vivid
part in the action.

In *Ghosts* Ibsen projects a whole series of crises in the
earlier lives of the characters. In the first year of her marriage, Mrs. Alving ran away from her husband and offered
herself to Manders, but he forced her to return to her
home; when her child was born, she had to "fight doubly
hard—fight a desperate fight so that no one should know

the sort of a man my child's father was"; she was soon faced with another crisis: her husband had an illegitimate child, by the servant in her own house; then she made another desperate decision: she sent her son away at the age of seven and never permitted him to return during the father's life. On her husband's death, she decided to build and endow an orphanage as a tribute to the memory of the man she hated poisonously.

One is amazed at the concreteness of these events. The construction is powerful and the detailed action is sharply visualized. The limit of the play's outer framework is Mrs. Alving's marriage. Ibsen regarded the family as the basic unit of society. The root-action of *Ghosts,* in which Mrs. Alving must decide whether or not to kill her own son, raises a question which the author cannot answer; it brings us face to face with the social necessity which defines and unifies the action. The marriage marks the beginning, and the ultimate extension, of the whole scheme. The essence of the root-action lies in Oswald's question: "I never asked you for life. And what kind of a life was it that you gave me?"

The concentrated conflict of will which is projected in the stage-action begins with Oswald's return from abroad. At this point the wills become conscious and active: the conflict does not involve an attempt to change the fixed structure of the family; it is a conflict with lesser necessities in order to bring them in line with this greater necessity; the family, purged of vice and deceit and disease, is the goal toward which the characters are struggling and the test of the value of their actions.

In *Hamlet* the limit of the action's extension is the poisoning of Hamlet's father, which the author presents in visual action through the device of the play within the play. The problem with which Shakespeare is concerned (and which had immediate social significance in his time) is the *release of the will* in action. The ability to act decisively and without inhibitions was vital to the men of the Renaissance who were challenging the fixed values of feudalism. When Hamlet says, "Thus conscience does make cowards of us all," he expresses the force of ideas and restrictions which are as real as the "ghosts of beliefs" of which Mrs.

Alving speaks. The outer framework therefore presents a system of events created by the passion and greed of people of strong wills. This is Hamlet's world, to the necessities of which he *must* adjust himself. Thus a deed of violence constitutes both the end and the beginning of the action and defines its scope.

On the other hand, the stage-action begins with the entry of the ghost; this is the point at which Hamlet's conscious will is awakened and directed toward a defined aim. The ghost represents the justification of the aim; he tells Hamlet that he is free to commit this act *within* the framework of social necessity. He tells him that the act is required in order to preserve the integrity of the family. But the conception of the family is changing; this accounts for Hamlet's confusion, for his inability to release his will; his affection for his mother blinds him, he cannot wreak quick vengeance on her, and yet he cannot understand her; he is puzzled by the "rank corruption, mining all within" which defiles the society in which he lives. He turns both to his mother and to Ophelia for help and both of them fail him, because both are dependent, financially and morally, on the men to whom they are attached. This, too, is part of the "iron framework of fact" which Hamlet must face. The root-action shows Hamlet conforming to necessity and dying to accomplish his aim; his last words are devoted solely to the world of action—

> I cannot live to hear the news from England;
> But I do prophesy the election lights
> On Fortinbras: he has my dying voice.

The process of selection is fundamentally a process of historical analysis. There is a direct analogy between the work of the dramatist and the work of the historian; the playwright cannot handle his material satisfactorily if his approach is personal or aesthetic; on the other hand, the emphasis on social forces is likely to be abstract. His work is greatly aided by the study of historical events and the utilization of an historical method. . . .

Fifty years ago, biographies of great men showed . . . heroes performing noble deeds and thinking high thoughts against a fixed background. Today the method of history and biography has undergone a great change. It is recognized that a satisfactory biography must show the individual in relation to the whole epoch. The tendency toward scandal and debunking is a minor indication of this trend: as a substitute for making the person real in terms of his time, he is made partially real in terms of his vices.

In dealing with an epoch, the historian (like the playwright) is faced with a problem of selection: he must investigate personal anecdotes, works of imagination and fact, journalistic comment, military and civil records. He must find a pattern of causation in this material. The pattern is dictated by the historian's conception of the meaning of the events; the interconnection and progression (the view of history as a process rather than as an isolated collection of meaningless incidents) depend on the historian's judgment of values, his idea of the aim of the process.

If one examines an historical event, or group of events, one finds that it is necessary to define the scope of the given action. In order to understand the American revolutionary war, one must co-ordinate the action in terms of the issue —the victory of the colonies—or in terms of some larger and later issue. If we regard the end of the war as the scope of the action, this throws a certain light upon every incident of the conflict. It gives a key to the logic of events, and also gives them color and texture. Both in a dramatic and in a military sense, Valley Forge gains a special meaning from Yorktown.

One cannot deal with a single incident in the American revolution without considering the complex forces involved: the personalities of the leaders, the aims of the American middle class, the property relations in the colonies, the libertarian ideas of the period, the tactics of the opposing armies. This does not mean that one presents a confusing or overbalanced picture. It means that the selection is made with an understanding of the relation between the parts and the whole.

Suppose one chooses to examine one of the less heroic and more personal aspects of the American war of independence: for instance, Benedict Arnold's personal tragedy. Can one consider his act of treason dramatically without considering the history of his time? One of the most significant things about Benedict Arnold's death is the fact that if he had died a little sooner he would have been the greatest hero of the war; the things which made him a traitor were closely connected with the things which motivated the desperate magnificence of his march to Quebec. This is a fascinating personal conflict, but it is as mad as a tale told by an idiot unless we know the historical background, the social forces which made the revolution, Arnold's relation to these forces, what the revolution meant to him, the culture and morals of his class.

The playwright may properly assume that he is dealing with a segment of history (regardless of whether his story is based on fact or invention). The playwright who feels that his characters are not as *historical* as Benedict Arnold, that they are more detached and less directly entangled in the whirlpool of history, is simply unfair to his characters and the situations in which he places them.

Is one, then, to make no distinction between plays which deal with known facts or famous personages, and those which concern intimate domestic problems? This is exactly my point. In both cases, the playwright must understand his characters in relation to their period.

This does not mean that the play itself must contain references and incidents which cover too wide an area. The whole point of selection is to be selective; the base of the action must be broad and solid—the action itself may involve a meticulous choice of incidents.

In the theatre today, the tendency is toward plays which are built, as it were, on stilts, which have no appreciable base. On the other hand, the younger and more socially-minded dramatists, eager to show us the width and depth of events, go to the other extreme. . . .

One can find many examples of historical method in plays which are not at all sweeping in their action, but which deal with limited domestic situations. For instance two English plays of the early nineteen-hundreds have considerable historical scope: *Chains,* by Elizabeth Baker (1909), and *Hindle Wakes,* by Stanley Houghton (1912). These are not great plays; they lack great depth or insight;

nevertheless both are solidly built on a workmanlike understanding of the social forces of the period.

Fanny's independence in *Hindle Wakes,* her flouting of
the moral code, has far less social meaning than Nora's
declaration of independence in *A Doll's House.* Nevertheless, Fanny is an historic figure; her attitude toward the
male, her integrity, her lack of depth, her cheerful assur-
ance that she can defeat the world—these are the qualities
of thousands of girls like Fanny; her rebellion, in 1912,
foreshadows the widespread rebellion, the brave but futile
gestures of the Greenwich Village era. When Fanny refuses
to marry Alan, who is the father of the child she is expecting, he says, "I know why you won't marry me." She says,
"Do you? Well, spit it out, lad." Alan: "You don't want to
spoil my life." Fanny: "Thanks, much obliged for the
compliment."

It is interesting to compare this with Shaw's treatment of
sex in *Man and Superman,* in which he shows us the
"eternal" woman in pursuit of her "eternal" mate. Shaw's
discussions, in spite of their brilliance, are always general,
and his characterizations are static, because he never
achieves historical perspective. *Hindle Wakes* is set realistically against the background of the 1912 era: the weav-
ing industry, the paternalism of the employers, the economic problems, the class relationships.

This is equally true of *Chains,* a carefully documented
picture of lower middle-class English life in 1909. The
business and home atmosphere, the habits, finances, and culture, the futile desire to escape, are exhibited with almost
scientific precision. . . .

A comparison between two plays by S. N. Behrman
illuminates the question of the historical framework as it
affects the technique of the drawing-room play. *Biography*
and *Rain From Heaven* are identical in theme. Based upon
the same conception, the difference lies solely in the process
of selection.

Both plays deal with the problem of the liberal in
modern society: in both the central figure is a woman of
culture, vividly honest, outspoken, tolerant. In both the
woman falls in love with a man who is involved in the

hate and bitterness of current social struggles. In both the
climax is the same: the intense love story comes to a
point of inevitable separation. The woman is emotionally
torn, but she is true to herself. She cannot relinquish her
tolerance, and she cannot change the man she loves.

In *Biography,* the historical groundwork is neglected.
The social forces which underlie the action have no
dramatic reality. As a result, the scope of the action is so
narrow that there can be no progression; the conflict between Marion Froude and Richard Kurt is repetitious
because it is based on fixed qualities of character. The
basis of the conflict is the same in the last scene as in the
first. Marion describes herself as "a big laissez-faire girl."
Marion evidently had this attitude in her youth, because
she tells Leander Nolan, with whom she had her first
affair, "I suspected in myself a—a tendency to explore,
a spiritual and physical wanderlust—that I knew would
horrify you once you found it out. It horrifies you now
when we are no longer anything to each other." Behrman
characterizes his heroine very carefully, but it is perfectly
evident that he does not view her in process of "becoming." Whatever might have caused Marion's "spiritual and
physical wanderlust," and how it might be affected by the
world in which Marion lives—these matters are rigorously
excluded from the play. During the course of the action,
she comes in contact with outside forces, but this contact
merely exposes the difference of aims between her and
Nolan and the boy with whom she falls in love. In her final
scene with Kurt, she says, "You hate my essential quality
—the thing that is me." So this core of personality is
static; it is in the final analysis mystical, and therefore un-
touchable. In a stage direction, the author speaks of "the
vast, uncrossable deserts between the souls of human
beings." Since these imaginary "deserts" are assumed to
exist, it follows that the actual contacts of the characters
are limited and sentimental.

Kurt's background contains an explanation of his point
of view; he tells Marion of the incident in his childhood
which motivates his bitterness; since this incident is a
genuine dramatization of social forces, it leads to the
most moving moment of the play, the love scene which

closes the second act. But there is no further development in Kurt's character, nor is the possibility of further development indicated.

Behrman tries to convince us that the social relationships presented in the stage-action have more than their apparent extension and meaning. Marion tries to explain Kurt's social point of view: "To you these rather ineffectual blundering people symbolize the forces that have hurt you and you hate them." This shows that the author's intentions are clear. This is what the people ought to do—but they cannot do it as *symbols;* the social forces can only be presented through crucial events.

The selection of events is confusing, and serves to weaken rather than develop the meaning of the root-action. Marion has gained considerable reputation painting the portraits of famous Europeans. Richard Kurt is a young radical who is editor of a weekly magazine, with a circulation of three million. These personal backgrounds do not serve to initiate a serious conflict of wills; Marion's career suggests Bohemianism and courage; it does *not* suggest any great degree of honesty and tolerance which (as we are repeatedly told) are Marion's essential qualities. Kurt presents a much more curious contradiction: how can a man who is an uncompromising radical be the editor of a periodical with three million circulation? This is never explained. It follows that the stage-action resolves itself into the discussion of an incident which has no social extension; Kurt wants to print Marion's autobiography because it will be sensational. The suggestion that the autobiography will serve any social purpose is an absurdity. We are told that Kurt is "only really at home in protest," but in a day of hunger marches, mass unemployment, threats of fascism and war, his protest consists in editing one of the largest magazines in the country and printing the mildly scandalous story of a woman's life.

In *Rain From Heaven,* Behrman attacks the same theme; but he has grown to a more mature consciousness of the social forces which motivate the conflict. The framework is not complete; there remains a tendency toward generalizations, and toward events which are illustrative rather than dramatic. But the root-action goes to the heart of a

genuine problem; the concept of social necessity is defined
and explored. Lady Wyngate is not an artificial Bohemian;
she is a genuine liberal; she knows what is going on in
the world and she tries to do something about it. Hugo
Willens is a refugee from Hitler's Germany. Lady Wyngate sees that her world is falling in ruins and she faces
the fact bravely. There are no "uncrossable deserts" in this
play; there are living problems—the threat of fascism, the
growing racial prejudice against the Jews, the desperation
of capitalism, the drive toward war. When the two lovers
face each other, and Hugo decides to return to Germany
to enter the struggle against fascism, the decision is an
honest act of will.

It is valuable to trace the detailed selection of incidents
in these two plays: it is literally true that every line and
situation depends on the way in which the social framework has been conceived. Hobart Eldridge, the financier
in *Rain From Heaven,* is simply a revision of Orrin Kinnicott in *Biography.* Kinnicott bears a satirical resemblance
to Bernarr MacFadden, but his point of view is not clearly
presented. In *Rain From Heaven,* the financier ceases to
be a caricature and becomes a character, because his activity is meaningful in social terms. Eldridge is doing exactly
what men of his sort are doing: he is helping to organize
fascism, and is doing it with a great deal of consciousness
and will.

In *Biography,* the complication in the love story is furnished by Nolan, who is engaged to Kinnicott's daughter
but is in love with Marion: Nolan is in politics and hopes
to become a Senator with the aid of the physical-culture
financier. In *Rain From Heaven,* the other man who is in
love with Lady Wyngate is Rand Eldridge. He is a combination of two characters from *Biography:* Nolan, and
Tympi Wilson, the handsome young movie actor who
appears briefly in the second act of *Biography.* When a
character makes what seems to be an entirely pointless appearance in a play, one may be sure that this character
represents some unrealized purpose in the back of the
playwright's mind. This is the case with Tympi; the dumb
popular movie hero turns up in *Rain From Heaven* as
the dumb popular hero of aviation; but he has acquired

vital meaning: he is the raw material of the Nazi storm troops. In *Biography* Nolan is a stuffy hypocrite. He has no basic connection with the heroine's problem. In *Rain From Heaven*, Behrman has developed and analyzed the character; in combining him with the young movie actor he has given him social meaning; as a result he becomes real, three-dimensional, a person with emotions and with a point of view.

The material in *Rain From Heaven* is not fully realized in terms of action. The construction is not compact. Behrman's remarkable knack for dialogue leads him into discursive discussions and incidents. The fact that the play deals so abstractly with contemporary issues is due to a one-sided approach to these issues; the idea of a destiny which overrides and paralyzes the human will influences Behrman's method, leading him to treat the total environment as an unknown and final power; the decisions of the characters are jerky and incomplete; the impact of social forces is shown in talk rather than in its deeper effect on the consciousness and will. The characters are not fully realized; they have certain qualities which cause them to struggle against the environment, but the roots of these qualities are not exposed. We have noted these tendencies in Shaw; similar modes of thought give a Shavian flavor to Behrman's technique.

Since the theme is not fully thought out, the various actions of the play have only a vague connection with the root-action. The various subsidiary stories are tangential, and are not unified in terms of climax. The final separation of the lovers is genuinely moving, but it is inconclusive. It is not the supreme moment of an inevitable struggle, in which the deepest motives and feelings have been dramatized. Being only partially developed, the situation is only partially effective in terms of theatre.

The tendency to regard external forces (social, moral, political, or psychological) as final manifestations of destiny, is characteristic of the modern man's relationship to his environment. Since one cannot dramatize the environment as something which is static or obscure, an abstract treatment of external forces destroys the validity of the play's social framework. One finds this weakness in many plays dealing with the struggles of the working class; social change is viewed mechanically or metaphysically, as if it were accomplished by some rational inevitability or dynamic life force greater than the totality of the wills involved.

In an authors' note to *1931*—Claire and Paul Sifton tell us that the play is "concerned with an individual in the tidal movement of a people caught in a situation which they can neither explain, escape, or develop." Perhaps it is unfair to say that this phraseology suggests O'Neill's "conflicting tides in the soul of man." But certainly "the tidal movement of a people" is made up of individual and collective attempts to "explain, escape, or develop"; where these attempts are absent there can be no tidal movement at all. The stage directions for the first scene of *1931*—speak of "the ebb of weariness, despair, blind pointless boredom, and subconscious desperation." If the authors had attempted to project anything of this sort, their play would be undramatic; but a great deal of the movement of the drama is vibrantly alive and defiant. However the conflict lacks depth; its extension is limited; the framework is too abstract to give the events their proper perspective.

In the first scene, Adam is fired from his job as a trucker in a warehouse. He expresses his conscious strength and will; he flexes his powerful muscles: "Look at that. That's beans, that's ham-and. That's women, that's gasoline. That's *everything*. I got it. I can lift more boxes, more iron, more sacks, load 'em faster, check 'em better, make more trips, do more work, than any of your damn . . ."—and he goes to face the world. But as Adam's will breaks, as he and the girl are crushed, the idea of a blind "tidal movement of people" tends to mechanize the action. Since the social forces are not accurately visualized, the psychological pressure is also vague. We are not permitted to see what is going on in the minds of the two central characters; they drift, unable to "explain, escape, or develop." At the end, when Adam says, "Might as well see what those guys outside are after. . . . Christ, I hope it's something I can get hold of with my hands," we cannot guess what this means in terms of character. The decision is not crucial, because the picture of reality has been documentary rather than fundamental; the decision remains an incident rather than an explosive change of equilibrium.

Yellow Jack, Sidney Howard's most noteworthy contribution to the theatre,* is a remarkable example of historical selection covering a wide field of events. Howard's perspective has definite limitations. But *Yellow Jack* has a scope which is rare in the theatre. This is undoubtedly due in some measure to the character of the subject matter. Dealing with the development of medical science during a period of its most intensive growth, Howard seems to have been deeply stirred by the possibilities of the material. The greatness of the theme impelled Howard to find an appropriate method of presentation. On the other hand, he might very easily have treated the subject in an unhistorical way: as the struggle of great "detached" individuals; or as a local-color story, drawing heavily upon the atmosphere of Cuba in 1900; or as a story of duty, self-sacrifice, and passion, with an intense love affair between Miss Blake and Carroll. These suggestions are not farfetched; these are the methods of the modern stage. It is amazing that Howard has, in one play, freed himself from these methods, and made some progress toward a broader technique.

In speaking of a broader technique, I am not referring to the physical arrangement of the stage in *Yellow Jack.* Howard explains in a note that "the play flows in a constantly shifting rhythm of light." This is an effective way of integrating the movement of the scenes, and was brilliantly realized in Jo Mielziner's set and Guthrie McClintic's production. But a playwright's technical achievement is not measured by whether his play is in one scene or forty, or whether he uses a constructivist set or a drawing room. The emphasis on the exterior trappings of a production is one of the more foolish manifestations of the old form-and-content argument. The number and kind of settings are dictated by the needs of the action; the playwright must also be guided, as Aristotle advised

---

* Written in collaboration with Paul de Kruif.

him, by consideration for the limitations of the playhouse. Howard might have restricted the movement of *Yellow Jack* to a single conventional set without restricting the historical scope.

The important thing about *Yellow Jack* is its attempt to treat the fight against yellow fever as a *process,* a conflict in which both individuals and a whole epoch are concerned. Howard's limitation lies in his emphasis on certain factors in the environment, and the neglect of other lines of causation. This springs from the habit of mind which was analyzed in the discussion of *The Silver Cord.* Just as in the former play, the scientific revelations of psychoanalysis are transformed into a "scientific Nemesis," so in *Yellow Jack* the power of medical science is idealized and made cosmic. The author is somewhat dazzled by the idea of "pure" science, detached from the interplay of social and economic forces.

This inability to grasp the whole of his material is evident in the final scene of the play. Here the conception of man's fight for science should be expressed in terms of the deepest and most crucial conflict: yet the last scene is static; Stackpoole, in his laboratory in London in 1929, is *explaining* rather than fighting: "Reed took the disease from monkey to man, Stokes took it from man to monkey. Now we shall be taking it from monkey back to man." It may be said that this is a summing up, that the core of the action concerns the events in Cuba in 1900. But a summing up cannot be less dramatic than the events of which it is the sum.

Yellow Jack reaches its climax in the scene in which the experiment on the four privates is completed. But this climax is sustained and carried over into the short scenes which follow. In the scene of the experiment, the author has been very careful to avoid bringing the action to a moment of maximum tension, thus permitting the action to build through the following scenes, in West Africa and London. One may say that it is the intention of these final scenes to show that the fight for science goes on. But this is the essence of the play. The author does not wish to tell us that the fight for science goes on, but that it grows *less* important and *less* dramatic. The final moments therefore should have been very fully dramatized.

The first scene of exposition takes place in Stackpoole's laboratory in London, in January, 1929, and we return to this same laboratory in the final scene. This opening is the logical point for the beginning of the stage-action. By opening in 1929, the dramatist shows us the *routine* of modern medical research in which mortal danger is treated with heroic unconcern. From this the action progresses to the dramatic struggles of the past; we see the increasing emotional force and meaning of the struggle as men fight slowly to conquer the deadly germ.

But if we examine the first scene carefully, we find that it contains many ideas which are never developed in the course of the play. These ideas are of the utmost importance; they are elements of the social framework which are essential to our complete understanding of the action; since they are introduced in this incomplete form, they constitute mere hints which have no concrete value.

The introductory scene starts with an argument between Stackpoole and a Major of the Royal Air Force and an official of the Kenya Colony. The officials are objecting to the six-day quarantine for plane passengers from West Africa going to Europe. The playwright is aware that Imperialism is in conflict with "pure" science in the year 1929; he is feeling his way toward some use of this conception. But he has not been able to crystallize this problem dramatically. This weakens the framework of causation; it narrows the scope of the events in Cuba in 1900; we cannot understand science in relation to man's life and aspirations unless we understand the social and economic forces which affect the development of science. There is evidently a connection between the British governmental pressure in regard to the Kenya colony and the economic interests of the United States in Cuba. But this remains an association of ideas in the playwright's mind and is never explained.

The climax exposes the conceptual uncertainty: a lonely scientist talks to himself in a vacuum. Stackpoole's final speech casts its shadow over every scene in the play; the action is weakened by the fact that the root-action is not given its full emotional force or extension.

The dominant principle which guides the process of selection is the principle that the play's explosive force can be no greater than the extension, the social implications, of the action. The social framework, however vast it may be, is of no value unless it meets the requirements of dramatic action: it must be concrete, defined, progressive.

The development of the stage-action is a further process of selection and arrangement; the concentrated analysis and projection of events within the social framework. This is a matter of more detailed structural problems; having determined the dynamic forces which underlie the play's movement, the playwright turns to the mechanics of construction.

EUGENE O'NEILL

Nobel Prize Address

FIRST, I wish to express again to you my deep regret that circumstances have made it impossible for me to visit Sweden in time for the festival, and to be present at this banquet to tell you in person of my grateful appreciation.

It is difficult to put into anything like adequate words the profound gratitude I feel for the greatest honor that my work could ever hope to attain—the award of the Nobel Prize. This highest of distinctions is all the more grateful to me because I feel so deeply that it is not only my work which is being honored, but the work of all my colleagues in America—that this Nobel Prize is a symbol of the recognition by Europe of the coming-of-age of the American theatre. For my plays are merely, through luck of time and circumstance, the most widely-known examples of the work done by American playwrights in the years since the World War—work that has finally made modern American drama in its finest aspects an achievement of which Americans can be justly proud, worthy at last to claim kinship with the modern drama of Europe, from which our original inspiration so surely derives.

This thought of original inspiration brings me to what is, for me, the greatest happiness this occasion affords, and that is the opportunity it gives me to acknowledge, with gratitude and pride, to you and to the people of Sweden, the debt my work owes to that greatest genius of all modern dramatists, your August Strindberg. It was reading his plays when I first started to write back in the winter of 1913-14 that, above all else, first gave me the vision of what modern

Reprinted with the permission of Carlotta Monterey O'Neill. First published in *The New York Times* of December 11, 1936.

41

drama could be, and first inspired me with the urge to write for the theatre myself. If there is anything of lasting worth in my work, it is due to that original impulse from him, which has continued as my inspiration down all the years since then—to the ambition I received then to follow in the footsteps of his genius as worthily as my talent might permit, and with the same integrity of purpose.

Of course, it will be no news to you in Sweden that my work owes much to the influence of Strindberg. That influence runs clearly through more than a few of my plays and is plain for everyone to see. Neither will it be news for anyone who has ever known me, for I have always stressed it myself. I have never been one of those who are so timidly uncertain of their own contribution that they feel they cannot afford to admit ever having been influenced, lest they be discovered as lacking all originality.

No, I am only too proud of my debt to Strindberg, only too happy to have this opportunity of proclaiming it to his people. For me, he remains, as Nietzsche remains in his sphere, the Master, still to this day more modern than any of us, still our leader. And it is my pride to imagine that perhaps his spirit, musing over this year's Nobel award for literature, may smile with a little satisfaction, and find the follower not too unworthy of his Master.

MAXWELL ANDERSON

The Essence of Tragedy

ANYBODY who dares to discuss the making of tragedy lays himself open to critical assault and general barrage, for the theorists have been hunting for the essence of tragedy since Aristotle without entire success. There is no doubt that playwrights have occasionally written tragedy successfully, from Aeschylus on, and there is no doubt that Aristotle came very close to a definition of what tragedy is in his famous passage on catharsis. But why the performance of a tragedy should have a cleansing effect on the audience, why an audience is willing to listen to tragedy, why tragedy has a place in the education of men, has never, to my knowledge, been convincingly stated. I must begin by saying that I have not solved the Sphinx's riddle which fifty generations of skillful brains have left in shadow. But I have one suggestion which I think might lead to a solution if it were put to laboratory tests by those who know something about philosophical analysis and dialectic.

There seems no way to get at this suggestion except through a reference to my own adventures in playwriting, so I ask your tolerance while I use myself as an instance. A man who has written successful plays is usually supposed to know something about the theory of playwriting, and perhaps he usually does. In my own case, however, I must confess that I came into the theatre unexpectedly, without preparation, and stayed in it because I had a certain amount of rather accidental success. It was not until after I had fumbled my way through a good many successes and an appalling number of failures that I began to doubt the sufficiency of dramatic instinct and to wonder whether or not there were general laws governing dramatic structure which so poor a head for theory as my own might grasp and use. I had read the *Poetics* long before I tried playwriting, and I had looked doubtfully into a few well-known handbooks on dramatic structure, but the maxims and theories propounded always drifted by me in a luminous haze—brilliant, true, profound in context, yet quite without meaning for me when I considered the plan for a play or tried to clarify an emotion in dialogue. So far as I could make out, every play was a new problem, and the old rules were inapplicable. There were so many rules, so many landmarks, so many pitfalls, so many essential reckonings, that it seemed impossible to find your way through the jungle except by plunging ahead, trusting to your sense of direction and keeping your wits about you as you went.

But as the seasons went by and my failures fell as regularly as the leaves in autumn, I began to search again among the theorists of the past for a word of wisdom that might take some of the gamble out of playwriting. What I needed most of all, I felt, was a working definition of what a play is, or perhaps a formula which would include all the elements necessary to a play structure. A play is almost always, probably, an attempt to recapture a vision for the stage. But when you are working in the theatre it's most unsatisfactory to follow the gleam without a compass, quite risky to trust "the light that never was on sea or land" without making sure beforehand that you are not being led straight into a slough of despond. In other words you must make a choice among visions, and you must check your chosen vision carefully before assuming that it will make a play. But by what rules, what maps, what fields of reference can you check so intangible a substance as a revelation, a dream, an inspiration, or any similar nudge from the subconscious mind?

I shan't trouble you with the details of my search for a criterion, partly because I can't remember it in detail. But I reread Aristotle's *Poetics* in the light of some bitter experience, and one of his observations led me to a comparison of ancient and modern playwriting methods. In discussing construction he made a point of the recognition scene as essential to tragedy. The recognition scene, as Aristotle isolated it in the tragedies of the Greeks, was generally an artificial device, a central scene in which the leading character saw through a disguise, recognized as a friend or as an enemy, perhaps as a lover or a member of his own family, some person whose identity had been hidden. Iphigenia, for example, acting as priestess in an alien country, receives a victim for sacrifice and then recognizes her own brother in this victim. There is an instant and profound emotional reaction, instantly her direction in the play is altered. But occasionally, in the greatest of the plays, the recognition turned on a situation far more convincing, though no less contrived. Oedipus, hunting savagely for the criminal who has brought the plague upon Thebes, discovers that he is himself that criminal—and since this is a discovery that affects not only the physical well-being and happiness of the hero, but the whole structure of his life, the effect on him and on the direction of the story is incalculably greater than could result from the more superficial revelation made to Iphigenia.

Now scenes of exactly this sort are rare in the modern drama except in detective stories adapted for the stage. But when I probed a little more deeply into the memorable pieces of Shakespeare's theatre and our own I began to see that though modern recognition scenes are subtler and harder to find, they are none the less present in the plays we choose to remember. They seldom have to do with anything so naïve as disguise or the unveiling of a personal identity. But the element of discovery is just as important as ever. For the mainspring in the mechanism of a modern play is almost invariably a discovery by the hero of some element in his environment or in his own soul of which he has not been aware—or which he has not taken sufficiently into account. Moreover, nearly every teacher of playwriting has had some inkling of this, though it was not until after I had worked out my own theory that what they said on this point took on accurate meaning for me. I still think that the rule which I formulated for my own guidance is more concise than any other, and so I give it here: A play should lead up to and away from a central crisis, and this crisis should consist in a discovery by the leading character which has an indelible effect on his thought and emotion and completely alters his course of action. The leading character, let me say again, must make the discovery; it must affect him emotionally; and it must alter his direction in the play.

Try that formula on any play you think worthy of study, and you will find that, with few exceptions, it follows this pattern or some variation of this pattern. The turning point of *The Green Pastures,* for example, is the discovery of God, who is the leading character, that even he must learn and grow, that a God who is to endure must conform to the laws of change. The turning point of *Hamlet* is Hamlet's discovery, in the play scene, that his uncle was unquestionably the murderer of his father. In *Abe Lincoln in Illinois* Lincoln's discovery is that he has been a coward, that he has stayed out of the fight for the Union because he was afraid. In each case, you will note, the discovery has a profound emotional effect on the hero, and gives an entirely new direction to his action in the play.

I'm not writing a disquisition on playwriting and wouldn't be competent to write one, but I do want to make a point of the superlative usefulness of this one touchstone for play structure. When a man sets out to write a play his first problem is his subject and the possibilities of that subject as a story to be projected from the stage. His choice of subject matter is his personal problem, and one that takes its answer from his personal relation to his times. But if he wants to know a possible play subject when he finds it, if he wants to know how to mold the subject into play form after he has found it, I doubt that he'll ever discover another standard as satisfactory as the modern version of Aristotle which I have suggested. If the plot he has in mind does not contain a playable episode in which the hero or heroine makes an emotional discovery, a discovery that practically dictates the end of the story, then such an episode must be inserted—and if no place can be found for it, the subject is almost certainly a poor one for the theatre. If this emotional discovery is contained in the story, but is not central, then it must be made central, and the whole action must revolve around it. In a three-act play it should fall near the end of the second act, though it may be delayed till the last; in a five-act play it will usually be found near the end of the third, though here also it can be delayed. Everything else in the play should be subordinated to this one episode—should lead up to or away from it.

Now this prime rule has a corollary which is just as important as the rule itself. The hero who is to make the central discovery in a play must not be a perfect man. He must have some variation of what Aristotle calls a tragic fault—and the reason he must have it is that when he makes his discovery he must change both in himself and in his action—and he must change for the better. The fault can be a very simple one—a mere unawareness, for example—but if he has no fault he cannot change for the better, but only for the worse, and for a reason which I shall discuss later, it is necessary that he must become more admirable, and not less so, at the end of the play. In other words, a hero must pass through an experience which opens his eyes to an error of his own. He must learn through suffering. In a tragedy he suffers death itself as a consequence of his fault or his attempt to correct it, but before he dies he has become a nobler person because of his recognition of his fault and the consequent alteration of his course of action. In a serious play which does not end in death he suffers a lesser punishment, but the pattern remains the same. In both forms he has a fault to begin with, he discovers that fault during the course of the action, and he does what he can to rectify it at the end. In *The Green Pastures* God's fault was that he believed himself perfect. He discovered that he was not perfect, and he resolved to change and grow. Hamlet's fault was that he could not make up his mind to act. He offers many excuses for his indecision until he discovers that there is no real reason for hesitation and that he has delayed out of cowardice. Lincoln, in *Abe Lincoln in Illinois,* has exactly the same difficulty. In the climactic scene it is revealed to him that he had hesitated to take sides through fear of the consequences to himself, and he then chooses to go ahead without regard for what may be in store for him. From the point of view of the playwright, then, the essence of a tragedy, or even of a serious play, is the spiritual awakening, or regeneration, of his hero.

When a playwright attempts to reverse the formula, when his hero makes a discovery which has an evil effect, or one which the audience interprets as evil, on his character, the play is inevitably a failure on the stage. In *Troilus and Cressida* Troilus discovers that Cressida is a light woman. He draws from her defection the inference that all women are faithless—that faith in woman is the possession of fools. As a consequence he turns away from life and seeks death in a cause as empty as the love he has given up, the cause of the strumpet Helen. All the glory of Shakespeare's verse cannot rescue the play for an audience, and save in *Macbeth* Shakespeare nowhere wrote so richly, so wisely, or with such a flow of brilliant metaphor.

For the audience will always insist that the alteration in the hero be for the better—or for what it believes to be the better. As audiences change, the standards of good and evil change, though slowly and unpredictably, and the meanings of plays change with the centuries. One thing only is certain: that an audience watching a play will go along with it only when the leading character responds in the end to what it considers a higher moral impulse than moved him at the beginning of the story, though the audience will of course define morality as it pleases and in the terms of its own day. It may be that there is no absolute up or down in this world, but the race believes that there is, and will not hear of any denial.

And now at last I come to the point toward which I've been struggling so laboriously. Why does the audi-

ence come to the theatre to look on while an imaginary
hero is put to an imaginary trial and comes out of it with
credit to the race and to himself? It was this question that
prompted my essay, and unless I've been led astray by my
own predilections there is a very possible answer in the
rules for playwriting which I have just cited. The theatre
originated in two complementary religious ceremonies, one
celebrating the animal in man and one celebrating the god.
Old Greek Comedy was dedicated to the spirits of lust and
riot and earth, spirits which are certainly necessary to the
health and continuance of the race. Greek tragedy was
dedicated to man's aspiration, to his kinship with the
gods, to his unending, blind attempt to lift himself above
his lusts and his pure animalism into a world where there
are other values than pleasure and survival. However un-
aware of it we may be, our theatre has followed the Greek
patterns with no change in essence, from Aristophanes and
Euripides to our own day. Our more ribald musical
comedies are simply our approximation of the Bacchic
rites of Old Comedy. In the rest of our theatre we sometimes follow Sophocles, whose tragedy is always an exaltation of the human spirit, sometimes Euripides, whose tragi-
comedy follows the same pattern of an excellence achieved
through suffering. The forms of both tragedy and comedy
have changed a good deal in nonessentials, but in essentials
—and especially in the core of meaning which they must
have for audiences—they are in the main the same religious rites which grew up around the altars of Attica
long ago.

It is for this reason that when you write for the theatre
you must choose between your version of a phallic revel
and your vision of what mankind may or should become.
Your vision may be faulty, or shallow, or sentimental, but
it must conform to some aspiration in the audience, or
the audience will reject it. Old Comedy, the celebration of
the animal in us, still has a place in our theatre, as it had
in Athens, but here, as there, that part of the theatre which
celebrated man's virtue and his regeneration in hours of
crisis is accepted as having the more important function.
Our comedy is largely the Greek New Comedy, which
grew out of Euripides' tragi-comedy, and is separated from

tragedy only in that it presents a happier scene and puts its protagonist through an ordeal which is less than lethal.

And since our plays, aside from those which are basically Old Comedy, are exaltations of the human spirit, since that is what an audience expects when it comes to the theatre, the playwright gradually discovers, as he puts plays before audiences, that he must follow the ancient Aristotelian rule: he must build his plot around a scene wherein his hero discovers some mortal frailty or stupidity in himself and faces life armed with a new wisdom. He must so arrange his story that it will prove to the audience that men pass through suffering purified, that, animal though we are, despicable though we are in many ways, there is in us all some divine, incalculable fire that urges us to be better than we are.

It could be argued that what the audience demands of a hero is only conformity to race morality, to the code which seems to the spectators most likely to make for race survival. In many cases, especially in comedy, and obviously in the comedy of Molière, this is true. But in the majority of ancient and modern plays it seems to me that what the audience wants to believe is that men have a desire to break the molds of earth which encase them and claim a kinship with a higher morality than that which hems them in. The rebellion of Antigone, who breaks the laws of men through adherence to a higher law of affection, the rebellion of Prometheus, who breaks the law of the gods to bring fire to men, the rebellion of God in *The Green Pastures* against the rigid doctrine of the Old Testament, the rebellion of Tony in *They Knew What They Wanted* against the convention that called on him to repudiate his cuckold child, the rebellion of Liliom against the heavenly law which asked him to betray his own integrity and make a hypocrisy of his affection, even the repudiation of the old forms and the affirmation of new by the heroes of Ibsen and Shaw, these are all instances to me of the groping of men toward an excellence dimly apprehended, seldom possible of definition. They are evidence to me that the theatre at its best is a religious affirmation, an age-old rite restating and reassuring man's belief in his own destiny and his ultimate hope. The theatre is much older than the doctrine of evolution, but its one faith, asseverated again and again for every age and every year, is a faith in evolution, in the reaching and the climb of men toward distant goals, glimpsed but never seen, perhaps never achieved, or achieved only to be passed impatiently on the way to a more distant horizon.

THORNTON WILDER

Some Thoughts on Playwriting

FOUR fundamental conditions of the drama separate it from the other arts. Each of these conditions has its advantages and disadvantages, each requires a particular aptitude from the dramatist, and from each there are a number of instructive consequences to be derived. These conditions are:

1. The theatre is an art which reposes upon the work of many collaborators.
2. It is addressed to the group-mind.
3. It is based upon a pretense and its very nature calls out a multiplication of pretenses.
4. Its action takes place in a perpetual present time.

I. THE THEATRE IS AN ART WHICH REPOSES UPON THE WORK OF MANY COLLABORATORS.

We have been accustomed to think that a work of art is by definition the product of one governing selecting will.

A landscape by Cézanne consists of thousands of brush-strokes, each commanded by one mind. *Paradise Lost* and *Pride and Prejudice,* even in cheap frayed copies, bear the immediate and exclusive message of one intelligence.

It is true that in musical performance we meet with intervening executants, but the element of intervention is slight compared to that which takes place in drama. Illustrations:

From *The Intent of the Artist.* Copyright © 1941 by Princeton University Press. Reprinted by permission of Brandt & Brandt. The essay is to be found on pp. 83–98 of this volume edited by Augusto Centeno.

1. One of the finest productions of *The Merchant of Venice* in our time showed Sir Henry Irving as Shylock, a noble, wronged, and indignant being, of such stature that the Merchants of Venice dwindled before him into irresponsible schoolboys. He was confronted in court by a gracious, even queenly, Portia, Miss Ellen Terry. At the Odéon in Paris, however, Gémier played Shylock as a vengeful and hysterical buffoon, confronted in court by a Portia who was a *gamine* from the Paris streets with a lawyer's quill three feet long over her ear; at the close of the trial scene Shylock was driven screaming about the auditorium, behind the spectators' backs and onto the stage again, in a wild Elizabethan revel. Yet for all their divergences both were admirable productions of the play.

2. If there were ever a play in which fidelity to the author's requirements were essential in the representation of the principal rôle, it would seem to be Ibsen's *Hedda Gabler,* for the play is primarily an exposition of her character. Ibsen's directions read: "Enter from the left Hedda Gabler. She is a woman of twenty-nine. Her face and figure show great refinement and distinction. Her complexion is pale and opaque. Her steel-gray eyes express an unruffled calm. Her hair is of an attractive medium brown, but is not particularly abundant; and she is dressed in a flowing loose-fitting morning gown." I once saw Eleonora Duse in this rôle. She was a woman of sixty and made no effort to conceal it. Her complexion was pale and transparent. Her hair was white, and she was dressed in a gown that suggested some medieval empress in mourning. And the performance was very fine.

One may well ask: why write for the theatre at all? Why not work in the novel where such deviations from one's intentions cannot take place?

There are two answers:

1. The theatre presents certain vitalities of its own so inviting and stimulating that the writer is willing to receive them in compensation for this inevitable variation from an exact image.

2. The dramatist through working in the theatre gradually learns not merely to take account of the presence of the collaborators, but to derive advantage from them;

and he learns, above all, to organize the play in such a way that its strength lies not in appearances beyond his control, but in the succession of events and in the unfolding of an idea, in narration.

The gathered audience sits in a darkened room, one end of which is lighted. The nature of the transaction at which it is gazing is a succession of events illustrating a general idea—the stirring of the idea; the gradual feeding out of information; the shock and countershock of circumstances; the flow of action; the interruption of action; the moments of allusion to earlier events; the preparation of surprise, dread, or delight—all that is the author's and his alone.

For reasons to be discussed later—the expectancy of the group-mind, the problem of time on the stage, the absence of the narrator, the element of pretense—the theatre carries the art of narration to a higher power than the novel or the epic poem. The theatre is unfolding action and in the disposition of events the authors may exercise a governance so complete that the distortions effected by the physical appearance of actors, by the fancies of scene-painters and the misunderstandings of directors, fall into relative insignificance. It is just because the theatre is an art of many collaborators, with the constant danger of grave misinterpretation, that the dramatist learns to turn his attention to the laws of narration, its logic and its deep necessity of presenting a unifying idea stronger than its mere collection of happenings. The dramatist must be by instinct a storyteller.

There is something mysterious about the endowment of the storyteller. Some very great writers possessed very little of it, and some others, lightly esteemed, possessed it in so large a measure that their books survive down the ages, to the confusion of severer critics. Alexandre Dumas had it to an extraordinary degree; while Melville, for all his splendid quality, had it barely sufficiently to raise his work from the realm of nonfiction. It springs, not, as some have said, from an aversion to general ideas, but from an instinctive coupling of idea and illustration; the idea, for a born storyteller, can only be expressed imbedded in its circumstantial illustration. The myth, the parable, the fable are the fountainhead of all fiction and in them is seen most clearly the didactic, moralizing employment of a story. Modern taste shrinks from emphasizing the central idea that hides behind the fiction, but it exists there nevertheless, supplying the unity to fantasizing, and offering a justification to what otherwise we would repudiate as mere arbitrary contrivance, pretentious lying, or individualistic emotional association-spinning. For all their magnificent intellectual endowment, George Meredith and George Eliot were not born storytellers; they chose fiction as the vehicle for their reflections, and the passing of time is revealing their error in that choice. Jane Austen was pure storyteller and her works are outlasting those of apparently more formidable rivals. The theatre is more exacting than the novel in regard to this faculty and its presence constitutes a force which compensates the dramatist for the deviations which are introduced into his work by the presence of his collaborators.

The chief of these collaborators are the actors.

The actor's gift is a combination of three separate faculties or endowments. Their presence to a high degree in any one person is extremely rare, although the ambition to possess them is common. Those who rise to the height of the profession represent a selection and a struggle for survival in one of the most difficult and cruel of the artistic activities. The three endowments that compose the gift are observation, imagination, and physical co-ordination.

1. An observant and analyzing eye for all modes of behavior about us, for dress and manner, and for the signs of thought and emotion in one's self and in others.

2. The strength of imagination and memory whereby the actor may, at the indication in the author's text, explore his store of observations and represent the details of appearance and the intensity of the emotions—joy, fear, surprise, grief, love, and hatred, and through imagination extend them to intenser degrees and to differing characterizations.

3. A physical co-ordination whereby the force of these inner realizations may be communicated to voice, face, and body.

An actor must *know* the appearances and the mental

states; he must *apply* his knowledge to the rôle; and he must physically *express* his knowledge. Moreover, his concentration must be so great that he can effect this representation under conditions of peculiar difficulty—in abrupt transition from the nonimaginative conditions behind the stage; and in the presence of fellow actors who may be momentarily destroying the reality of the action.

A dramatist prepares the characterization of his personages in such a way that it will take advantage of the actor's gift.

Characterization in a novel is presented by the author's dogmatic assertion that the personage was such, and by an analysis of the personage with generally an account of his or her past. Since in the drama, this is replaced by the actual presence of the personage before us and since there is no occasion for the intervening all-knowing author to instruct us as to his or her inner nature, a far greater share is given in a play to (1) highly characteristic utterances and (2) concrete occasions in which the character defines itself under action and (3) a conscious preparation of the text whereby the actor may build upon the suggestions in the rôle according to his own abilities.

Characterization in a play is like a blank check which the dramatist accords to the actor for him to fill in—not entirely blank, for a number of indications of individuality are already there, but to a far less definite and absolute degree than in the novel.

The dramatist's principal interest being the movement of the story, he is willing to resign the more detailed aspects of characterization to the actor and is often rewarded beyond his expectation.

The sleepwalking scene from *Macbeth* is a highly compressed selection of words whereby despair and remorse rise to the surface of indirect confession. It is to be assumed that had Shakespeare lived to see what the genius of Sarah Siddons could pour into the scene from that combination of observation, self-knowledge, imagination, and representational skill, even he might have exclaimed, "I never knew I wrote so well!"

II. THE THEATRE IS AN ART ADDRESSED TO A GROUP-MIND.

Painting, sculpture, and the literature of the book are certainly solitary experiences; and it is likely that most people would agree that the audience seated shoulder to shoulder in a concert hall is not an essential element in musical enjoyment.

But a play presupposes a crowd. The reasons for this go deeper than (1) the economic necessity for the support of the play and (2) the fact that the temperament of actors is proverbially dependent on group attention.

It rests on the fact that (1) the pretense, the fiction, on the stage would fall to pieces and absurdity without the support accorded to it by a crowd, and (2) the excitement induced by pretending a fragment of life is such that it partakes of ritual and festival, and requires a throng.

Similarly the fiction that royal personages are of a mysteriously different nature from other people requires audiences, levées, and processions for its maintenance. Since the beginnings of society, satirists have occupied themselves with the descriptions of kings and queens in their intimacy and delighted in showing how the prerogatives of royalty become absurd when the crowd is not present to extend to them the enhancement of an imaginative awe.

The theatre partakes of the nature of festival. Life imitated is life raised to a higher power. In the case of comedy, the vitality of these pretended surprises, deceptions, and *contretemps* becomes so lively that before a spectator, solitary or regarding himself as solitary, the structure of so much event would inevitably expose the artificiality of the attempt and ring hollow and unjustified; and in the case of tragedy, the accumulation of woe and apprehension would soon fall short of conviction. All actors know the disturbing sensation of playing before a handful of spectators at a dress rehearsal or performance where only their interest in pure craftsmanship can barely sustain them. During the last rehearsals the phrase is often heard: "This play is hungry for an audience."

Since the theatre is directed to a group-mind, a number of consequences follow:

1. A group-mind presupposes, if not a lowering of standards, a broadening of the fields of interest. The other arts may presuppose an audience of connoisseurs trained in leisure and capable of being interested in certain rarefied aspects of life. The dramatist may be prevented from exhibiting, for example, detailed representations of certain moments in history that require specialized knowledge in the audience, or psychological states in the personages which are of insufficient general interest to evoke self-identification in the majority. In the Second Part of Goethe's *Faust* there are long passages dealing with the theory of paper money. The exposition of the nature of misanthropy (so much more drastic than Molière's) in Shakespeare's *Timon of Athens* has never been a success. The dramatist accepts this limitation in subject matter and realizes that the group-mind imposes upon him the necessity of treating material understandable by the larger number.

2. It is the presence of the group-mind that brings another requirement to the theatre—forward movement.

Maeterlinck said that there was more drama in the spectacle of an old man seated by a table than in the majority of plays offered to the public. He was juggling with the various meanings in the word "drama." In the sense whereby drama means the intensified concentration of life's diversity and significance he may well have been right; if he meant drama as a theatrical representation before an audience he was wrong. Drama on the stage is inseparable from forward movement, from action.

Many attempts have been made to present Plato's dialogues, Gobineau's fine series of dialogues, *La Renaissance,* and the *Imaginary Conversations* of Landor; but without success. Through some ingredient in the group-mind, and through the sheer weight of anticipation involved in the dressing-up and the assumption of fictional rôles, an action is required, and an action that is more than a mere progress in argumentation and debate.

III. THE THEATRE IS A WORLD OF PRETENSE.

It lives by conventions: a convention is an agreed-upon falsehood, a permitted lie.

Illustrations: Consider at the first performance of the *Medea*, the passage where Medea meditates the murder of her children. An anecdote from antiquity tells us that the audience was so moved by this passage that considerable disturbance took place.

The following conventions were involved:

1. Medea was played by a man.
2. He wore a large mask on his face. In the lip of the mask was an acoustical device for projecting the voice. On his feet he wore shoes with soles and heels half a foot high.
3. His costume was so designed that it conveyed to the audience, by convention: woman of royal birth and oriental origin.
4. The passage was in metric speech. All poetry is an "agreed-upon falsehood" in regard to speech.
5. The lines were sung in a kind of recitative. All opera involves this "permitted lie" in regard to speech.

Modern taste would say that the passage would convey much greater pathos if a woman "like Medea" had delivered it—with an uncovered face that exhibited all the emotions she was undergoing. For the Greeks, however, there was no pretense that Medea was on the stage. The mask, the costume, the mode of declamation, were a series of signs which the spectator interpreted and reassembled in his own mind. Medea was being re-created within the imagination of each of the spectators.

The history of the theatre shows us that in its greatest ages the stage employed the greatest number of conventions. The stage is fundamental pretense and it thrives on the acceptance of that fact and in the multiplication of additional pretenses. When it tries to assert that the personages in the action "really are," really inhabit such and such rooms, really suffer such and such emotions, it loses rather than gains credibility. The modern world is inclined to laugh condescendingly at the fact that in the plays of Racine and Corneille the gods and heroes of antiquity were dressed like the courtiers under Louis XIV; that in the Elizabethan age scenery was replaced by placards notifying the audience of the location; and that a whip in the

hand and a jogging motion of the body indicated that a
man was on horseback in the Chinese theatre; these devices did not spring from naïveté, however, but from the
vitality of the public imagination in those days and from
an instinctive feeling as to where the essential and where
the inessential lay in drama.

The convention has two functions:

1. It provokes the collaborative activity of the spectator's
   imagination; and
2. It raises the action from the specific to the general.

This second aspect is of even greater importance than
the first.

If Juliet is represented as a girl "very like Juliet"—it
was not merely a deference to contemporary prejudices
that assigned this rôle to a boy in the Elizabethan age—
moving about in a "real" house with marble staircases,
rugs, lamps, and furniture, the impression is irresistibly
conveyed that these events happened to this one girl, in
one place, at one moment in time. When the play is staged
as Shakespeare intended it, the bareness of the stage re-
leases the events from the particular and the experience
of Juliet partakes of that of all girls in love, in every time,
place, and language.

The stage continually strains to tell this generalized
truth and it is the element of pretense that reinforces it.
Out of the lie, the pretense, of the theatre proceeds a
truth more compelling than the novel can attain, for the
novel by its own laws is constrained to tell of an action
that "once happened"—"once upon a time."

IV. THE ACTION ON THE STAGE TAKES PLACE IN A PERPETUAL PRESENT TIME.

Novels are written in the past tense. The characters in
them, it is true, are represented as living moment by moment their present time, but the constant running commen-
tary of the novelist ("Tess slowly descended into the
valley"; "Anna Karenina laughed") inevitably conveys to
the reader the fact that these events are long since past
and over.

The novel is a past reported in the present. On the stage it is always now. This confers upon the action an increased vitality which the novelist longs in vain to incorporate into his work.

This condition in the theatre brings with it another important element:

In the theatre we are not aware of the intervening storyteller. The speeches arise from the characters in an apparently pure spontaneity.

A play is what takes place.

A novel is what one person tells us took place.

A play visibly represents pure existing. A novel is what one mind, claiming to omniscience, asserts to have existed.

Many dramatists have regretted this absence of the narrator from the stage, with his point of view, his powers of analyzing the behavior of the characters, his ability to interfere and supply further facts about the past, about simultaneous actions not visible on the stage, and above *all* his function of pointing the moral and emphasizing the significance of the action. In some periods of the theatre he has been present as chorus, or prologue and epilogue, or as raisonneur. But surely this absence constitutes an additional force to the form, as well as an additional tax upon the writer's skill. It is the task of the dramatist so to coordinate his play, through the selection of episodes and speeches, that though he is himself not visible, his point of view and his governing intention will impose themselves on the spectator's attention, not as dogmatic assertion or motto, but as self-evident truth and inevitable deduction.

Imaginative narration—the invention of souls and destinies—is to a philosopher an all but indefensible activity.

Its justification lies in the fact that the communication of ideas from one mind to another inevitably reaches the point where exposition passes into illustration, into parable, metaphor, allegory, and myth.

It is no accident that when Plato arrived at the height of his argument and attempted to convey a theory of knowledge and a theory of the structure of man's nature he passed over into storytelling, into the myths of the Cave and the Charioteer; and that the great religious teachers have constantly had recourse to the parable as a means of imparting their deepest intuitions.

The theatre offers to imaginative narration its highest possibilities. It has many pitfalls and its very vitality betrays it into service as mere diversion and the enhancement of insignificant matter; but it is well to remember that it was the theatre that rose to the highest place during those epochs that aftertime has chosen to call "great ages" and that the Athens of Pericles and the reigns of Elizabeth, Philip II, and Louis XIV were also the ages that gave to the world the greatest dramas it has known.

On a Streetcar Named Success

SOME time this month I will observe the third anniversary of the Chicago opening of *The Glass Menagerie,* an event which terminated one part of my life and began another about as different in all external circumstances as could be well imagined. I was snatched out of virtual oblivion and thrust into sudden prominence, and from the precarious tenancy of furnished rooms about the country I was removed to a suite in a first-class Manhattan hotel. My experience was not unique. Success has often come that abruptly into the lives of Americans.

No, my experience was not exceptional, but neither was it quite ordinary, and if you are willing to accept the somewhat eclectic proposition that I had not been writing with such an experience in mind—and many people are not willing to believe that a playwright is interested in anything but popular success—there may be some point in comparing the two estates.

The sort of life which I had had previous to this popular success was one that required endurance, a life of clawing and scratching along a sheer surface and holding on tight with raw fingers to every inch of rock higher than the one caught hold of before, but it was a good life because it was the sort of life for which the human organism is created.

I was not aware of how much vital energy had gone into this struggle until the struggle was removed. I was out on a level plateau with my arms still thrashing and my lungs

Permission granted by The New York Times to reprint "On a Streetcar Named Success" by Tennessee Williams from *The New York Times* of November 30, 1947.

still grabbing at air that no longer resisted. This was security at last.

I sat down and looked about me and was suddenly very depressed. I thought to myself, this is just a period of adjustment. Tomorrow morning I will wake up in this first-class hotel suite above the discreet hum of an East Side boulevard and I will appreciate its elegance and luxuriate in its comforts and know that I have arrived at our American plan of Olympus. Tomorrow morning when I look at the green satin sofa I will fall in love with it. It is only temporarily that the green satin looks like slime on stagnant water.

But in the morning the inoffensive little sofa looked more revolting than the night before and I was already getting too fat for the $125 suit which a fashionable acquaintance had selected for me. In the suite things began to break accidentally. An arm came off the sofa. Cigarette burns appeared on the polished surfaces of the furniture. Windows were left open and a rainstorm flooded the suite. But the maid always put it straight and the patience of the management was inexhaustible. Late parties could not offend them seriously. Nothing short of a demolition bomb seemed to bother my neighbors.

I lived on room-service. But in this, too, there was a disenchantment. Sometime between the moment when I ordered dinner over the phone and when it was rolled into my living room like a corpse on a rubber-wheeled table, I lost all interest in it. Once I ordered a sirloin steak and a chocolate sundae, but everything was so cunningly disguised on the table that I mistook the chocolate sauce for gravy and poured it over the sirloin steak.

Of course all this was the more trivial aspect of a spiritual dislocation that began to manifest itself in far more disturbing ways. I soon found myself becoming indifferent to people. A well of cynicism rose in me. Conversations all sounded like they had been recorded years ago and were being played back on a turntable. Sincerity and kindliness seemed to have gone out of my friends' voices. I suspected them of hypocrisy. I stopped calling them, stopped seeing them. I was impatient of what I took to be inane flattery.

I got so sick of hearing people say, "I loved your play!" that I could not say thank you any more. I choked on the words and turned rudely away from the usually sincere person. I no longer felt any pride in the play itself but began to dislike it, probably because I felt too lifeless inside ever to create another. I was walking around dead in my shoes, and I knew it but there was no one I knew or trusted sufficiently, at that time, to take him aside and tell him what was the matter.

This curious condition persisted about three months, till late spring, when I decided to have another eye operation, mainly because of the excuse it gave me to withdraw from the world behind a gauze mask. It was my fourth eye operation, and perhaps I should explain that I had been afflicted for about five years with a cataract on my left eye which required a series of needling operations and finally an operation on the muscle of the eye. (The eye is still in my head. So much for that.)

Well, the gauze mask served a purpose. While I was resting in the hospital the friends whom I had neglected or affronted in one way or another began to call on me and now that I was in pain and darkness, their voices seemed to have changed, or rather that unpleasant mutation which I had suspected earlier in the season had now disappeared and they sounded now as they used to sound in the lamented days of my obscurity. Once more they were sincere and kindly voices with the ring of truth in them.

When the gauze mask was removed I found myself in a readjusted world. I checked out of the handsome suite at the first-class hotel, packed my papers and a few incidental belongings, and left for Mexico, an elemental country where you can quickly forget the false dignities and conceits imposed by success, a country where vagrants innocent as children curl up to sleep on the pavements and human voices, especially when their language is not familiar to the ear, are soft as birds'. My public self, that artifice of mirrors, did not exist here and so my natural being was resumed.

Then, as a final act of restoration, I settled for a while at Chapala to work on a play called *The Poker Night,* which later became *A Streetcar Named Desire.* It is only in his work that an artist can find reality and satisfaction, for the actual world is less intense than the world of his invention and consequently his life, without recourse to violent disorder, does not seem very substantial. The right condition for him is that in which his work is not only convenient but unavoidable.

This is an oversimplification. One does not escape that easily from the seductions of an effete way of life. You cannot arbitrarily say to yourself, I will now continue my life as it was before this thing, Success, happened to me. But once you fully apprehend the vacuity of a life without struggle you are equipped with the basic means of salvation. Once you know this is true, that the heart of man, his body, and his brain, are forged in a white-hot furnace for the purpose of conflict (the struggle of creation) and that with the conflict removed, the man is a sword cutting daisies, that not privation but luxury is the wolf at the door, and that the fangs of this wolf are all the little vanities and conceits and laxities that Success is heir to—why, then with this knowledge you are at least in a position of knowing where danger lies.

You know, then, that the public Somebody you are when you "have a name" is a fiction created with mirrors and that the only somebody worth being is the solitary and unseen you that existed from your first breath and which is the sum of your actions and so is constantly in a state of becoming under your own volition—and knowing these things, you can even survive the catastrophe of Success!

It is never altogether too late, unless you embrace the Bitch Goddess, as William James called her, with both arms and find in her smothering caresses exactly what the homesick little boy in you always wanted, absolute protection and utter effortlessness. Security is a kind of death, I think, and it can come to you in a storm of royalty checks beside a kidney-shaped pool in Beverly Hills or anywhere at all that is removed from the conditions that made you an artist, if that's what you are or were or intended to be. Ask anyone who has experienced the kind of success I am talking about—What good is it? Perhaps to get an honest answer you will have to give him a shot of truth-serum but the word he will finally groan is unprintable in genteel publications.

Then what is good? The obsessive interest in human affairs, plus a certain amount of compassion and moral conviction, that first made the experience of living something that must be translated into pigment or music or bodily movement or poetry or prose or anything that's dynamic and expressive—that's what's good for you if you're at all serious in your aims. William Saroyan wrote a great play on this theme, that purity of heart is the one success worth having. "In the time of your life—live!" That time is short and it doesn't return again. It is slipping away while I write this and while you read it, and the monosyllable of the clock is Loss, Loss, Loss, unless you devote your heart to its opposition.

PAUL GREEN

Symphonic Drama

I

MANY years ago I became interested in a Negro settlement on the outskirts of a certain Southern university town. This settlement consisted of four or five hundred people. It incorporated into itself almost everything good and bad, cruel and hopeful, superstitious and factual to be found in any village below the Mason and Dixon Line.

Here were the turgid upboiling and rich manifestations of humanity with all their special intensity of emotion, willfulness, and wild flarings of the imagination—manifestations which Negro folk life in America so fully provides. I dreamed and pondered over this settlement. I wanted to give dramatic expression to this environment and active milieu of life. I wanted to write a play about these people.

Certain decisions had to be made. A central gathering place must be established in the play—a place where the people would be brought in and where they could discharge their dramatic story message, where they could unload their personalities, as it were, in the scene and pass out and return to unload again.

What would the center be? First I thought of that gathering place of communal life, the church. But on consideration, it offered certain stiff and formal difficulties. Next I thought of the corner grocery store. But, owing to its pragmatic and definite purpose, I found it too narrow and confining. What about a barbecue stand? I could see the people eating there, hear their loud guffaws as jokes were cracked. See a quarrel being picked. There comes the strolling form of the Law. But, no, that won't do. Too many representatives of Negro life, especially the more delicate and feminine side of its society, would be excluded.

I finally chose a boarding-house—a proper-sized boarding-house. And for freedom of movement and contrasting mass of bodies and lights and shadows I would need several levels of playing action. Therefore a boarding-house with a porch on it. And, too, there should be a yard and some shade trees—one shade tree—in front. People in the South like to sit under shade trees. The walls of the rooms in this house should be opened so that the inner workings of this dwelling as a habiting place for human souls could be depicted as the story required. Also why not a lean-to at the back into which we could progue our sight? It could be a level higher than the room in front of it. This was good. And a bed in it also—always a dramatic and creative property.

And if necessary I could bring in another small center of action—the local barbershop shack. Yes, that would be right. So off at the left of the yard I moved a tiny outbuilding where the seeking light could cast its interested eye now and then and discover to the audience whatever bits of action might be needed to further the story along.

And let a street cross at the right where the moody and restless life of the people could pass in emphasis and illustration as the play required. So now I had enough of a home, with intimate cells, in which the dramatic honeybee could work.

The scene had four playing levels then—the yard, the front porch, the main interior of the house, and the higher lean-to level at the rear. In addition, there were the playing spot of the little barbershop outbuilding and the highway of action along the road to the right.

In and around this boarding-house I now collected my characters, some seventy-five or a hundred of them, all representative of a cross-section of Negro life. Among them were a preacher, a mother or two, a granny woman, a voodoo doctor, several convicts, a harlot, a beautician, a sport, a blind musician, several day laborers, cooks, an undertaker, several pairs of sweethearts, a salesman of death insurance—and men, women, and children. These last were in the main chorus figures. The theme I had in mind brought them all into being—and not the reverse.

What about the time? I must choose an hour and a day in which it would be natural for this Negro life to coagulate and congregate itself into such a setting. A Saturday night then. It must not be in winter, for then my characters could not do their stuff out of doors. So summer it must be—a warm summer night when one week's hard work had ended and another week's had not yet begun. At such a time the story germ would sprout quietly, develop normally, and break into a final bloom of explosiveness. Then after this, normal life would return to quiescence again and the play be over.

As I worked at the drama, I felt again and again that I was involved in the same sort of enterprise as a composer driving forward his composition for some eighty or a hundred instruments. The whole body of the work must be kept propelling itself onward by means of the individual instrumentations which came forward to personal fulfillment, returned, and gave place to others, and they in turn likewise. Motifs must be developed, thematic statements made and exploited, and a ferment of symphonic creativity be kept brewing to self-realization. And all to be sternly controlled by the architectonic power of the story line. Whatever failed to advance the story would not be used. For, after all, drama is storytelling. Of whatever sort, it is storytelling in action. Of course a little functional and lyrical decoration could be indulged in now and then. But only beauty spots, as it were, to be tinted in on the face of the whole.

And the *idée fixe,* say, as in a Beethoven or Berlioz symphony, the sensed and felt and inner natural form, call it even the melodic line, whether submerged or surfaced— must control matters.

The story line was a creature alive indeed. And even as the will-o'-the-wisp, he lived in and inhabited the scene.

There the little creature enters from the street. He moves about the yard. The house calls to him. He enters there. He takes possession of a room for a while, and the human beings indwelling there are disturbed and thrown into fits even at his galvanic appearance—an appearance called up out of their own deep desires and activities, their clashing wills and urges in themselves—just as the violins flutter and cry out in sweet stridency or joyful pain as the burden of the symphonic movement develops or comes to being in their vibrating and shaken bosoms.

II

I kept searching for a term of definition and interpretation to describe my play as I worked at it.

I found that in trying to express the inner lives and turmoilings of my Negro community I was having to call upon nearly all the available elements in modern theatrical art. And there were plenty of them. Folk song and poetry were needed here. Likewise the dance and pantomime and chorus voices. Even the mental speech of the grisly microphone and echo chamber could be used to get inside the soul life of some of my disturbed and vitalized people. Moments of horrification would call for masks. And ever there was the dynamic flow and modulation of light to accompany the human behavior at work. Light that would illuminate a volatile and advancing story point. And in that illumination the mind of the appreciator could read the message clear. The fabled fire in the Scriptures was like this light, the furnace fire in which the Hebrew children once stood all bright and glorified.

And always there was music—music!

"Music drama" didn't seem the right term for the play. "Ballad opera" it couldn't be. Nor "opera." "Festival play" was too loose and misnoming. "Lyric drama" lacked entirety. Finally "symphonic drama" seemed right. Yes, a "sounding-together" in the true meaning of the Greek word. The term seemed a little highfalutin, and I deplored that. But it was nearer what I wanted than anything else. And so I adopted it and have continued to use it for other like plays I have written since.

III

I found in writing this Negro drama that by the symphonic use of the various elements of the theatre, especially music, there came a freedom and fullness of possible story statement not otherwise to be had in dealing with large groups of people in action. Short cuts and intensifications could be quickly indulged in which the audience would accept without question. Conventions could be quickly established, and the story beginnings could be hatched out of an obstructive matrix without much ado.

In this kind of theatre, too, time could be telescoped through a symbol—even could become that symbol. Space might be compressed or expanded, say, like the breathing of some huge and delicate accordion of the mind. Tomorrow is already here. A voice of the inner chorus commentator out of the life of my Negro village could say so. And in the thickened moody and musically charmed environment, in the climate of credibility established, the audience would agree.

There was a nemesis in my Negro play. A huge and oncoming highway was being built by the white man across the earth and was aimed straight at this Negro settlement. The deep reverberations of dynamite exploding in the hills, clearing the way for this road, sounded ominously and constantly nearer as the drama proceeded.

Passions and hates and loves and fears and whorings were fecundating in this village. During the play murder was committed in the boarding-house. Then came the wham-wham of a policeman's stick, and the hoarse great voice of the Law was heard bellowing like Behemoth through the valley. Culprits and innocent ones ran this way and that in fear. The Golem tread of justice and retribution came nearer. The reverberations on the distant road sounded closer, louder. Nature herself became sick, upset, and violent. A fierce wind whoomed and whistled among the shacks in the valley and around our particular boarding-house. The limbs of the shade tree in the yard twisted and swung like a gesticulating maniac. A final and terrific explosion occurred in the street at the right. A pandemonium of shrieking and lamentations of the people rose in the valley! The moon dropped down the sky like a shot. And then, with the echoes falling away, the tumult and the terror died. The scene faded gently and musically out. From the darkness came a low and fervent chanted prayer of the persecuted and disordered people. A few heartbeats of time and no more, and the light swam up again.

The iron-snouted machine-age road had arrived. The nemesis was there. It had plowed its revengeful way through the settlement like a cruel steel coulter through an anthill. The old boarding-house had been pushed aside. The entrails of furniture and pieces of bedding spilled out along the torn earth. Because of the depravity, the sinfulness, and causeless misery of these sorrowful ones, the road had taken its toll.

A dozen or more striped convicts were working, digging away on this road now, slinging their picks and bringing them down, and ever bringing them down in the white blazing sun. The heat of August shimmered across the land. "Lazy Lawrence" danced his fiendish monkey dance in the sun. The sweat poured down, the only cooling dampness in the world for the mourners on that road. On a stump to the left a guard squatted, drowsy, vapid, like a toad. The rifle in the crook of his arm kept alert, its muzzle warned like an eye, it threatened. The convicts dug on and on, their faces set down the infinite stretch of cruel road that reached from the rising to the setting sun. And as their picks came down against the earth with a thud, a husky desperate groaning chant burst from their baked lips, carrying on and carrying on over the long deadening hours of pain.

In this form of symphonic drama the convicts and the digging had become the road.

The form seemed right then for the expression of such group life, of setting forth the relationships of individuals and their fellows, of masses and crowds affected, energized and motivated as they would be by some centripetal idea and dramatic intent—some story of tradition, of folk inheritance and legend, some famous native character or group of characters splurging themselves forth out of their heritage.

IV

So I wrote the piece to the best of my ability. Then began the peddling of it for Broadway. I experienced to the fullest the torturous way to production so often endured by American playwrights. I would have been much wiser of course to have found some amateur group and perfected the production with them first. But no, it must be Broadway or nothing, I thought. I have learned better since. Some half-dozen managers were intrigued by the play, bought it and owned it in turn, paying five hundred dollars down, fiddling with the script six months, and dropping it. For three years they did so. Finally one more foolhardy than the rest, a woman, undertook it.

The play arrived at the Cort Theatre on Forty-eighth Street in New York. From the beginning on that autumn night [October 2, 1934] everything went wrong. Our prize exhibit of twenty-two choral voices in the pit, flanked by a drum and a clarinet to provide the basic musical folk-stratum, went dead on that opening night. All its fire was doused. All sense of Negro revival participatingness had vanished. It was a cold group, frozen, stiff, automatic, and unable to fuse itself into the body of the play. And yet Dolphe Martin's score of notated vocables was sure and eager and alive.

The actors likewise played separate and aloof solitaire. The voice of the Almighty (the white man's Law), which had been placed high in the scenery aloft by means of a loudspeaker, blew a fuse in the midst of its stern admonition to the struggling and wayward Negro villagers. The already puzzled audience broke into laughter.

And all the while there was to be no relieving intermission. I had been bull-headed on this point. This was to be a through train, like the train that took old Daniel away in the song, and there would be no stopping until it arrived at its final destination, either heaven or hell.

It was to be hell.

I walked restlessly up and down in the lobby of the theatre. I kept going out to the sidewalk to see how the weather was up the narrow canyon of the dark sky and then back listening, waiting for any sound of encouraging applause from within the auditorium. None came out. But a man came out instead, irate, hot, and bothered. He was a big fellow and to my then disordered imagination looked like Goliath, and me with no slingshot and only a heart for a stone.

"Play or no play," he said, "I'm going to smoke."

It was Bob Benchley, and I knew we were sunk.

V

Two days later word was received that Mr. Shubert wanted his theatre come Saturday night for another show. Trembling and afraid, I went over to see him. He was gracious and humane and unsmiling.

"Your drama lacks entertainment," he said.

"But if we could only keep it going another week. Give it a chance. Maybe it would catch on. It's a sort of new form, you know. Atkinson's review was not bad. I have a wire here from him praising it. And Mrs. Isaacs of *Theatre Arts* thinks highly of it."

"I understand how you feel," he said, "but I already have another show booked to come into the Cort right away." His voice grew a little hard. "A full-length play without an intermission is unthinkable. The audience won't stand for it."

"Won't sit for it," I corrected inwardly.

I looked at his emotionless face. There was something familiar about him. Then I knew. It was his snow-white collar and his black exact tie. In the very play he was kicking out one of the characters was a Negro mortician. Mr. Shubert's collar and tie were identical with the Negro's and as solemn and unfeeling. The office was a morgue then, and I was glad to get away to fresh air. So *Roll Sweet Chariot* rolled out of the theatre on Saturday night into silence.

VI

I tried this sort of symphonic drama a couple of other times on Broadway. Once the cool and loyal judgment of Cheryl Crawford, the enthusiasm of Harold Clurman and the Group Theatre, the fine direction of Lee Strasberg and the resilient and theatre-wise music of Kurt Weill—all helped to mend matters. But they were not enough, and *Johnny Johnson* likewise was marked down as a failure. I still remember with appreciation though that the critics' circle gave it a tombstone vote of confidence for its obituary.

Then there was *Native Son,* which I co-authored with Richard Wright out of his dynamic and powerful novel of the same name. This play was symphonic in its use of music and musicalized sound effects especially. The undismayed personal dominance and theatricality of Mr. Orson Welles helped salvage the piece and drive it across to some sort of crippled success. It ran in New York for several months and then continued around on the road for a year or two. It is now being played in different parts of the world in various translations, and I hate to think that its meaning to foreign audiences is not its drama but its propaganda.

I have written several symphonic dramas away from Broadway and have had better success in staging them in outdoor theatres than in indoor ones. Down on lonely Roanoke Island in North Carolina Sir Walter Raleigh's colony perished in 1587. A hundred and twenty-one men, women, and children disappeared from the face of the earth without a whisper as to their fate. For many years I thought about this mystery as material for a symphonic drama. With local devotion and a great deal of WPA and Federal Theatre help we built an outdoor amphitheatre there close on the quiet waters of Roanoke Sound. And in a setting of yellow sands and live oak trees we opened *The Lost Colony* in 1937. The play is beginning its annual summer season and has already passed the 600th performance. Through these years hundreds of thousands of people have come to see this project in communal theatre and to hear the old English music, the folk song and hymn tunes of our musical heritage, and to see the native Indian dances—all part of the symphonic drama. The little fishing village of near-by Manteo furnishes us with many actors, New York likewise. They all meet here, more than a hundred of them, year after year, and put on this play, their play. And the miracle to me is that the box office has so far provided enough salary to give each participant a modest living wage.

Another symphonic drama already written is *The Highland Call*. It is designed for production in the Cape Fear Valley in North Carolina. This valley is a home and center of the Scottish settlement in the United States. And recently there among the tall pines outside the city of Fayetteville close by Fort Bragg we selected a site for our outdoor theatre. And here, before long, it is my hope, the story of the Scottish heroine, Flora Macdonald, with the music and ballads and dance of the early Scottish settlers in the New World, will be played nightly under the stars.

The Common Glory at Williamsburg, Virginia, is another example of this type of drama with which I have recently been working. This play covers six years in the life of Thomas Jefferson and is concerned mainly with his efforts to further the creation of democratic government in these United States. This summer will mark the seventh season of the drama. And so far it has been highly successful as regards attendance and box-office income. The policy of using local actors, strengthened by some Broadway professional ones, is used here just as in the case of *The Lost Colony* and the planned-for *The Highland Call*.

And there have been other symphonic dramas—*Faith of Our Fathers* produced in the beautiful outdoor theatre in Rock Creek Park, Washington, for the seasons of 1950 and 1951, *The 17th Star* produced at Columbus, Ohio, in the summer of 1953 in celebration of the state's sesquicentennial celebration, and *Serenata,* a fiesta drama of old Spanish days in Santa Barbara, with Josefina Niggli, the summer of 1953.

And waiting ahead is *The Shepherd of the Isles,* the drama of that great humanitarian James Oglethorpe and his settlements of Georgia, planned for production in a theatre to be built on St. Simon's Island in 1954. Then there is the story of the tenacious and pious pilgrims at Plymouth. After that, the drama of the trials and sufferings of the first settlers in that nightmare of terror that was Jamestown.

And up and down the length of California I have trav-

eled, stopping at every old mission from San Francisco to
San Diego looking for a site, a home for a future great
passion play of the Southwest. It seems now as if somewhere in the quiet and brooding mountains of Ojai Valley
a place will be found for building the most beautiful outdoor theatre in the world, and there under the dry and
rainless stars the religious and inspiring story of the early
padres in that wide land could be restated and relived.

VII

This type of drama which I have elected to call symphonic seems to be fitted to the needs and dramatic genius
of the American people. Our richness of tradition, our
imaginative folk life, our boundless enthusiasm and health,
our singing and dancing and poetry, our lifted hearts and
active feet and hands, even our multitudinous mechanical
and machine means for self-expression—all are too out-
pouring for the narrow confines of the usual professional
and killingly expensive Broadway play and stage. But they
can be put to use in the symphonic drama and its theatre.
It is wide enough, free enough, and among the people
cheap enough for their joy and use.

ARTHUR MILLER

Tragedy and the Common Man

IN THIS age few tragedies are written. It has often been held that the lack is due to a paucity of heroes among us, or else that modern man has had the blood drawn out of his organs of belief by the skepticism of science, and the heroic attack on life cannot feed on an attitude of reserve and circumspection. For one reason or another, we are often held to be below tragedy—or tragedy above us. The inevitable conclusion is, of course, that the tragic mode is archaic, fit only for the very highly placed, the kings or the kingly, and where this admission is not made in so many words it is most often implied.

I believe that the common man is as apt a subject for tragedy in its highest sense as kings were. On the face of it this ought to be obvious in the light of modern psychiatry, which bases its analysis upon classific formulations, such as the Oedipus and Orestes complexes, for intances, which were enacted by royal beings, but which apply to everyone in similar emotional situations.

More simply, when the question of tragedy in art is not at issue, we never hesitate to attribute to the well-placed and the exalted the very same mental processes as the lowly. And finally, if the exaltation of tragic action were truly a property of the high-bred character alone, it is inconceivable that the mass of mankind should cherish tragedy above all other forms, let alone be capable of understanding it.

As a general rule, to which there may be exceptions un-

known to me, I think the tragic feeling is evoked in us
when we are in the presence of a character who is ready
to lay down his life, if need be, to secure one thing—his
sense of personal dignity. From Orestes to Hamlet, Medea
to Macbeth, the underlying struggle is that of the individual attempting to gain his "rightful" position in his
society.

Sometimes he is one who has been displaced from it,
sometimes one who seeks to attain it for the first time, but
the fateful wound from which the inevitable events spiral
is the wound of indignity, and its dominant force is indignation. Tragedy, then, is the consequence of a man's total
compulsion to evaluate himself justly.

In the sense of having been initiated by the hero himself,
the tale always reveals what has been called his "tragic
flaw," a failing that is not peculiar to grand or elevated
characters. Nor is it necessarily a weakness. The flaw, or
crack in the character, is really nothing—and need be
nothing—but his inherent unwillingness to remain passive
in the face of what he conceives to be a challenge to his
dignity, his image of his rightful status. Only the passive,
only those who accept their lot without active retaliation,
are "flawless." Most of us are in that category.

There are among us today, as there always have been,
those who act against the scheme of things that degrades
them, and in the process of action everything we have accepted out of fear or insensitivity or ignorance is shaken
before us and examined, and from this total onslaught by
an individual against the seemingly stable cosmos sur-
rounding us—from this total examination of the "un-
changeable" environment—comes the terror and the fear
that is classically associated with tragedy.

More important, from this total questioning of what has
previously been unquestioned, we learn. And such a process
is not beyond the common man. In revolutions around the
world, these past thirty years, he has demonstrated again
and again this inner dynamic of all tragedy.

Insistence upon the rank of the tragic hero, or the so-
called nobility of his character, is really but a clinging to
the outward forms of tragedy. If rank or nobility of char-

acter was indispensable, then it would follow that the problems of those with rank were the particular problems of tragedy. But surely the right of one monarch to capture the domain of another no longer raises our passions, nor are our concepts of justice what they were to the mind of an Elizabethan king.

The quality in such plays that does shake us, however, derives from the underlying fear of being displaced, the disaster inherent in being torn away from our chosen image of what and who we are in this world. Among us today this fear is as strong, and perhaps stronger, than it ever was. In fact, it is the common man who knows this fear best.

Now, if it is true that tragedy is the consequence of a man's total compulsion to evaluate himself justly, his destruction in the attempt posits a wrong or an evil in his environment. And this is precisely the morality of tragedy and its lesson. The discovery of the moral law, which is what the enlightenment of tragedy consists of, is not the discovery of some abstract or metaphysical quantity.

The tragic right is a condition of life, a condition in which the human personality is able to flower and realize itself. The wrong is the condition which suppresses man, perverts the flowing out of his love and creative instinct. Tragedy enlightens—and it must, in that it points the heroic finger at the enemy of man's freedom. The thrust for freedom is the quality in tragedy which exalts. The revolutionary questioning of the stable environment is what terrifies. In no way is the common man debarred from such thoughts or such actions.

Seen in this light, our lack of tragedy may be partially accounted for by the turn which modern literature has taken toward the purely psychiatric view of life, or the purely sociological. If all our miseries, our indignities, are born and bred within our minds, then all action, let alone the heroic action, is obviously impossible. And if society alone is responsible for the cramping of our lives, then the protagonist must needs be so pure and faultless as to force us to deny his validity as a character. From neither of these views can tragedy derive, simply because neither represents a balanced concept of life. Above all else, tragedy requires the finest appreciation by the writer of cause and effect.

No tragedy can therefore come about when its author fears to question absolutely everything, when he regards any institution, habit, or custom as being either everlasting, immutable, or inevitable. In the tragic view the need of man to wholly realize himself is the only fixed star, and whatever it is that hedges his nature and lowers it is ripe for attack and examination. Which is not to say that tragedy must preach revolution.

The Greeks could probe the very heavenly origin of their ways and return to confirm the rightness of laws. And Job could face God in anger, demanding his right, and end in submission. But for a moment everything is in suspension, nothing is accepted, and in this stretching and tearing apart of the cosmos, in the very action of so doing, the character gains "size," the tragic stature which is spuriously attached to the royal or the highborn in our minds. The commonest of men may take on that stature to the extent of his willingness to throw all he has into the contest, the battle to secure his rightful place in his world.

There is a misconception of tragedy with which I have been struck in review after review, and in many conversations with writers and readers alike. It is the idea that tragedy is of necessity allied to pessimism. Even the dictionary says nothing more about the word than that it means a story with a sad or unhappy ending. This impression is so firmly fixed that I almost hesitate to claim that in truth tragedy implies more optimism in its author than does comedy, and that its final result ought to be the reinforcement of the onlooker's brightest opinions of the human animal.

For, if it is true to say that in essence the tragic hero is intent upon claiming his whole due as a personality, and if this struggle must be total and without reservation, then it automatically demonstrates the indestructible will of man to achieve his humanity.

The possibility of victory must be there in tragedy. Where pathos rules, where pathos is finally derived, a character has fought a battle he could not possibly have won. The pathetic is achieved when the protagonist is, by virtue of his witlessness, his insensitivity, or the very air he gives off, incapable of grappling with a much superior force.

Pathos truly is the mode for the pessimist. But tragedy requires a nicer balance between what is possible and what is impossible. And it is curious, although edifying, that the plays we revere, century after century, are the tragedies. In them, and in them alone, lies the belief—optimistic, if you will—in the perfectibility of man.

It is time, I think, that we who are without kings took up this bright thread of our history and followed it to the only place it can possibly lead in our time—the heart and spirit of the average man.

TENNESSEE WILLIAMS

The Timeless World of a Play

CARSON McCULLERS concludes one of her lyric poems with the line: "Time, the endless idiot, runs screaming 'round the world." It is this continual rush of time, so violent that it appears to be screaming, that deprives our actual lives of so much dignity and meaning, and it is, perhaps more than anything else, the *arrest of time* which has taken place in a completed work of art that gives to certain plays their feeling of depth and significance. In the London notices of *Death of a Salesman* a certain notoriously skeptical critic made the remark that Willy Loman was the sort of man that almost any member of the audience would have kicked out of an office had he applied for a job or detained one for conversation about his troubles. The remark itself possibly holds some truth. But the implication that Willy Loman is consequently a character with whom we have no reason to concern ourselves in drama, reveals a strikingly false conception of what plays are. Contemplation is something that exists outside of time, and so is the tragic sense. Even in the actual world of commerce, there exists in some persons a sensibility to the unfortunate situations of others, a capacity for concern and compassion, surviving from a more tender period of life outside the present whirling wire-cage of business activity. Facing Willy Loman across an office desk, meeting his nervous glance and hearing his querulous voice, we would be very likely to glance at our wrist watch and our schedule of other appointments. We would not kick him out of the office, no, but we would certainly *ease* him out with more expedition than Willy had feebly hoped for. But suppose there had been no wrist watch or office clock, and suppose there had *not* been the schedule of pressing appointments, and suppose that we were not actually facing Willy across a desk—and facing a person is *not* the best way to *see* him!—suppose, in other words, that the meeting with Willy Loman had somehow occurred in a world *outside* of time. Then I think we would receive him with concern and kindness and even with respect. If the world of a play did not offer us this occasion to view its characters under that special condition of a *world without time,* then, indeed, the characters and occurrences of drama would become equally pointless, equally trivial, as corresponding meetings and happenings in life.

The classic tragedies of Greece had tremendous nobility. The actors wore great masks, movements were formal, dance-like, and the speeches had an epic quality which doubtless were as removed from the normal conversation of their contemporary society as they seem today. Yet they did not seem false to the Greek audiences: the magnitude of the events and the passions aroused by them did not seem ridiculously out of proportion to common experience. And I wonder if this was not because the Greek audiences knew, instinctively or by training, that the created world of a play is removed from that element which makes people *little* and their emotions fairly inconsequential.

Great sculpture often follows the lines of the human body: yet the repose of great sculpture suddenly transmutes those human lines to something that has an absoluteness, a purity, a beauty, which would not be possible in a living mobile form.

A play may be violent, full of motion: yet it has that special kind of repose which allows contemplation and produces the climate in which tragic importance is a possible thing, provided that certain modern conditions are met.

In actual existence the moments of love are succeeded by the moments of satiety and sleep. The sincere remark is followed by a cynical distrust. Truth is fragmentary, at best: we love and betray each other not in quite the same breath but in two breaths that occur in fairly close sequence. But the fact that passion occurred in *passing,* that it then declined into a more familiar sense of indifference, should not be regarded as proof of its inconsequence. And this is the very truth that drama wishes to bring us. . . .

Whether or not we admit it to ourselves, we are all haunted by a truly awful sense of impermanence. I have always had a particularly keen sense of this at New York cocktail parties, and perhaps that is why I drink the martinis almost as fast as I can snatch them from the tray. This sense is the febrile thing that hangs in the air. Horror of insincerity, of *not meaning,* overhangs these affairs like the cloud of cigarette smoke and the hectic chatter. This horror is the only thing, almost, that is left unsaid at such functions. All social functions involving a group of people not intimately known to each other are always under this shadow. They are almost always (in an unconscious way) like that last dinner of the condemned: where steak or turkey, whatever the doomed man wants, is served in his cell as a mockingly cruel reminder of what the great-big-little-transitory world had to offer.

In a play, time is arrested in the sense of being confined. By a sort of legerdemain, events are made to remain *events,* rather than being reduced so quickly to mere *occurrences.* The audience can sit back in a comforting dusk to watch a world which is flooded with light and in which emotion and action have a dimension and dignity that they would likewise have in real existence, if only the shattering intrusion of time could be locked out.

About their lives people ought to remember that when they are finished, everything in them will be contained in a marvelous state of repose which is the same as that which they unconsciously admired in drama. The rush is temporary. The great and only possible dignity of man lies in his power deliberately to choose certain moral values by which to live as steadfastly as if he, too, like a character in a play, were immured against the corrupting rush of time. Snatching the eternal out of the desperately fleeting is the great magic trick of human existence. As far as we know, as far as there exists any kind of empiric evidence, there is no way to beat the game of *being* against *non-being,* in which non-being is the predestined victor on realistic levels.

Yet plays in the tragic tradition offer us a view of certain moral values in violent juxtaposition. Because we do not participate, except as spectators, we can view them clearly, within the limits of our emotional equipment. These people on the stage do not return our looks. We do not have to answer their questions nor make any sign of being in company with them, nor do we have to compete with their virtues nor resist their offenses. All at once, for this reason, we are able to *see* them! Our hearts are wrung by recognition and pity, so that the dusky shell of the auditorium where we are gathered anonymously together is flooded with an almost liquid warmth of unchecked human sympathies, relieved of self-consciousness, allowed to function. . . .

Men pity and love each other more deeply than they permit themselves to know. The moment after the phone has been hung up, the hand reaches for a scratch pad and scrawls a notation: "Funeral Tuesday at five, Church of the Holy Redeemer, don't forget flowers." And the same hand is only a little shakier than usual as it reaches, some minutes later, for a highball glass that will pour a stupefaction over the kindled nerves. Fear and evasion are the two little beasts that chase each other's tails in the revolving wire cage of our nervous world. They distract us from feeling too much about things. Time rushes toward us with its hospital tray of infinitely varied narcotics, even while it is preparing us for its inevitably fatal operation. . . .

So successfully have we disguised from ourselves the intensity of our own feelings, the sensibility of our own hearts, that plays in the tragic tradition have begun to seem untrue. For a couple of hours we may surrender ourselves to a world of fiercely illuminated values in conflict, but when the stage is covered and the auditorium lighted, almost immediately there is a recoil of disbelief. "Well, well!" we say as we shuffle back up the aisle, while the play dwindles behind us with the sudden perspective of an early Chirico painting. By the time we have arrived at Sardi's, if not as soon as we pass beneath the marquee, we have convinced ourselves once more that life has as little resemblance to the curiously stirring and meaningful occurrences on the stage as a jingle has to an elegy of Rilke.

This modern condition of his theatre audience is something that an author must know in advance. The diminishing influence of life's destroyer, time, must be somehow worked into the context of his play. Perhaps it is a certain foolery, a certain distortion toward the grotesque, which will solve the problem for him. Perhaps it is only restraint, putting a mute on the strings that would like to break all bounds. But almost surely, unless he contrives in some way to relate the dimensions of his tragedy to the dimensions of a world in which time is *included*—he will be left among his magnificent debris on a dark stage, muttering to himself: "Those fools. . . ."

And if they could hear him above the clatter of tongues, glasses, chinaware, and silver, they would give him this answer: "But you have shown us a world not ravaged by time. We admire your innocence. But we have seen our photographs, past and present. Yesterday evening we passed our first wife on the street. We smiled as we spoke but we didn't really see her! It's too bad, but we know what is true and not true, and at 3 A.M. your disgrace will be in print!"

WILLIAM INGE

The Schizophrenic Wonder

AN AUTHOR, particularly a playwright going through the ordeal of his first play, probably always feels that misunderstanding has accompanied the soul-satisfying understanding expressed in the varied reactions to his work. In the case of my play, *Come Back, Little Sheba,* I have found reactions so unpredictably split that I am inclined to regard the New York audience as a sort of schizophrenic wonder. Admiration, affection, confusion, dislike, indifference, and warm enthusiasm all have been expressed by reviewers for a play which at the time of writing I expected, perhaps as all writers expect, would have one sure effect on its spectators. After all opinions are voiced, the author is grateful for those who have understood and liked the play, who have reacted to it as he hoped people would; he wants to erase what he feels are misunderstandings about it, to clarify what he thought he was writing in contrast with what others thought he was writing; and to those who have expressed no liking, comprehension, or admiration at all, he wants to wave a farewell, as he might to people with whom he found, after a brief visit, no means of communication.

Come Back, Little Sheba is a play about a couple passing into middle age, dimly wondering where their youthful happiness has gone, looking tentatively in the future for something to replace it. But even Lola's youth was unfulfilled. Someone always stood between her and a fully realized happiness. She met Doc when he went to college. They had a courtship that lasted almost a year and for the

First published in *Theatre Arts,* XXXIV (May, 1950), 22–23, and reprinted here by permission of Ashley Famous Agency.

first time they both found they could sing and dance and laugh and make love like other young people. Then their new-found joy caught up with them and trapped them into a necessary marriage, forcing them into adjustments neither was equipped to make. Youth to Lola was a song that ended before she had quite learned the tune. Youth to Doc was a snare that tore him away from the straight, upward path to a future of security and respect. When Marie, a young college girl, rents a room in their house, youth is again in their midst. Doc sees in her the embodiment of all the high and perhaps false spiritual ideals he holds so dear in young womanhood, not because Marie possesses these qualities, but because he manufactures them for her. And Lola wants to live vicariously in Marie the youth she missed. She regards the girl somewhat more realistically than Doc, but neither of them is prepared to experience youth today. The casual, candid way Marie and Turk, the young athlete, accept a relation that is purely physical comes as a shock to the elders. Both finally are brought to their senses. Doc gets maniacally drunk and Lola almost loses her life. Then something happens inside them; they realize their dependence on each other; their love has made its first entrance into maturity.

Some reviewers felt, and I can see why they did, that Doc's unexpected outburst of drunken violence revealed a deeper inner conflict than the rest of the play in its presentation of him had prepared for; that if Doc actually were going to kill Lola, his wife, there must be a homicidal streak in his make-up which demands separate explanation and dramatic treatment. My answer here is that many innocent alcoholics, totally devoid of homicidal instincts or possessing no more of same than law-abiding citizens, have awakened in the morning and found themselves under arrest for murder. Doc *might* have killed Lola, but doing so would have been a sordid accident. The violence of the alcoholic usually misses, by subconscious intent, its destructive end. The alcoholic loves the display of violence. His violence is a childish protest against his own feelings of weakness. Still, there are homicidal men who are also alcoholic, men not necessarily alcoholic who murder when they are drunk. I feel the rest of the play establishes that Doc is none of these.

Of course *Sheba* is not a tragedy and I think the play misses its mark if it is regarded as such. One reviewer called it "a pathetic comedy" and I feel this is a happy classification. I felt that I was writing a comedy, hoping others would find it a rather lyrical play full of pathos, humor, melancholy, warmth, affection, and absurdity, with one painful stab of insight into a man's regret. I felt the play might have something in common, in character, with the terrifying but still humorous comedies of O'Casey, maybe with those of Chekhov.

Certainly, poor Doc and Lola could never begin to measure up to the proportions of tragic heroes. As people, Doc and Lola may point to vaster tragedies in the social background behind them, but I was concerned only with Doc and Lola themselves. I found them lovable, weak, warmhearted, foolish, naïve, a little pretentious, and only occasionally brave. Except for bravery, though on a full-time basis, these are not the characteristics that usually make up a tragic hero. We do not necessarily love Hamlet, or even Willy Loman in *Death of a Salesman,* nor do we sympathize with them; rather we understand the forces which would destroy them and are deeply moved by their inability to overcome them. Their tragedy lies not in the fact that they perish, but that they *must* perish; and the world, although it has not been able to sustain them, still will feel their loss. Doc and Lola are people the world was never aware of, but the world's ignorance doesn't make them any the more or less interesting and likable as human beings.

There are some clichés of criticism many critics, professional and amateur, feel they can righteously and safely make about plays. One of these springs from a suspicion of psychiatric overtones, particularly those dealing with dream symbolism. Any exposition of dream symbolism is regarded as phony, just as a dramatist's use of sociological, political, musical, and artistic references in a play usually have caused reviewers immediately to take for granted he is misinformed. All I can say is that, as far as I know, there is no established set of dream symbols one must go by, that the meaning of such symbols necessarily varies from one individual to another, that several psychiatrists read my script and gave their approval before I even submitted it, and finally that Lola's dreams have a *dramatic* function and purpose, I believe, whether a scientific one or not.

Some have complained that *Come Back, Little Sheba* is depressing. I can only answer that I am not aware of its being so. The ending is not a hopeless one by any means; I think there is cheer in Doc and Lola's sitting together at the kitchen table, coming to a new realization, after their near catastrophe, of their need for each other; coming perhaps to some shadowy realization of a possible new life together. Doc may or may not go on another binge; it is impossible to make predictions. I, for one, find it very easy to believe he will not. After all, he has given his life some shape, even though he seeks at times to destroy that shape; and he has established certain values and ideals it satisfies him to live up to. As for Lola, she is certainly as well off having fun with the postman and the milkman as she would be at bridge parties and teas. If she keeps a messy house, that is strictly her business and Doc doesn't seem to mind seriously. Their lives are not radiant with happiness and achievement, but they have found together a way to survive.

Doc, because he is pompous and self-righteous, should not fool people into regarding him as a fallen aristocrat who has married beneath his station. If Lola is uneducated, lax, and not very intelligent, she possesses enough human warmth and compassion to make her his equal in basic human worth. The only personal rancor I was induced to feel by reactions to the play was for those who carelessly referred to Lola as a "slut." The whole point of her character is that, despite her love of dreaming and disregard for household responsibilities (childish rather than slovenly), she is *not* a slut; she is essentially a very virginal, sincere, and honest woman. Nor is Marie a "slut." Surely we are thinking in very Victorian terms if we refer to a girl in this way just because she has been seduced before marriage. I cannot help thinking we still are unable to separate low morals from low incomes and perhaps low mentalities when we resort so abusively to such terms. The heroines of Maugham, Behrman, Barry, and the more recent T. S. Eliot are saved from such slander because their dramatists have surrounded them by environments in which "one simply does not use that kind of language."

Some objections have been made that the slow first act of *Come Back, Little Sheba* was indicative of the play's weak structure. This struck me as a somewhat arbitrary requirement to build the elements of the play, not according to the form most natural to them, but according to a form that has served perhaps far too many other Broadway plays. Form, to me, is the shape any creative work must take in order to exist with its ultimate force, beauty, and meaning. If the first act of *Sheba* moved more swiftly, more predictably, and with more indication of what is to come, Doc's outburst would not be the revelation it is. I feel that the audience, when Doc makes his drunken attack on Lola, should be shocked into incredibility, and then after a second's pause come to the realization it had to be.

I remember once being in a tornado. It came like a blast after a morning of unnatural quiet in the atmosphere. It wasn't a dull or monotonous quiet; it somehow had intensity and meaning, and there would be just an occasional breath of breeze to suggest a hidden restlessness that had to break. No one could interpret this atmosphere, but people in the community felt that something was going to happen. That is the atmosphere I wanted to create in my play: a slow, slightly suspenseful prelude to the eruption of a man's despair.

ROBINSON JEFFERS

The Tower Beyond Tragedy

EMERSON said, speaking of the ancient Greeks: "Our admiration of the antique is not admiration of the old, but of the natural." And likewise Ernest Renan: "The Greek miracle . . . a kind of eternal beauty, without any local or national taint."

I quote these sayings—whether or not they are quite accurate—because they express exactly the feeling that led me to write *The Tower Beyond Tragedy*. In making poems of contemporary life—this was more than twenty-five years ago—I had found my mood cramped by the conventions and probabilities of the time; particularly by our convention of understatement. It is our custom to avoid lyrical speech, and to express any great passion in whispers, or perhaps not at all. The human voice is a terrible organ, we must not extend it. To express a violent motion violently, or a beautiful one beautifully, would be shocking in daily life; but it is normal in Greek tragedy.

Certainly the Greeks, too, had their reticences and inhibitions—but different from ours, and they do not much concern us now—and perhaps the Greeks of prehistory did not. At least, according to tragic myth, they were singularly uninhibited in action. They represent elemental human nature, stripped—like Greek sculpture—of its neutral and unessential clothing: the customs and costumes that require attention in a story of contemporary life, or in any other period-piece.

The essay appeared first in *The New York Times* of November 26, 1950, and is reprinted here by permission of Jeffers Literary Properties.

This was my feeling when I wrote about Clytemnestra and Agamemnon. I don't remember clearly why that story in particular was chosen—except that it is one of the most dramatic in the world—but I think that photographs of the famous Lion-gate, and other prehistoric stone-work, still standing at Mycenae, had something to do with my choice; and I think also that the end of the poem—the experience of Orestes, which gives the poem its name—was present in my mind from the beginning; and was my first reason, or at least my best excuse, for writing.

I needed an excuse; I was a little ashamed to take two or three Greek tragedies, change them considerably, and make them into a poem. It seemed lazy and self-indulgent; for the story and the characters, except for my changes, were already created by better men than we are. Also it looked like neglect of duty to leave America and dream about ancient Greece; my proper business was not with antiquity. And I was not even assuming the disciplines of dramatic writing; the poem was not intended for the stage; some parts of it were frankly narrative. So I was glad to have something of my own to present at the end, though it is quite alien to Greek thought.

This was the pantheistic mysticism of Orestes, which comes to him like a religious conversion after he has committed his criminal act of justice. The house of Agamemnon is a wicked house, corrupted by power, heavy with ancestral crime and madness; of all its descendants only Orestes at last escapes the curse; he turns away from human lust and ambition to the cold glory of the universe.

A patriot may identify himself with his nation, or a saint with God; Orestes, in the poem, identifies himself with the whole divine nature of things; earth, man, and stars, the mountain forest and the running streams; they are all one existence, one organism. He perceives this, and that himself is included in it, identical with it. This perception is his tower beyond the reach of tragedy; because, whatever may happen, the great organism will remain forever immortal and immortally beautiful. Orestes has "fallen in love outward," not with a human creature, nor a limited cause, but with the universal God.

That is my meaning in the poem. It would probably sound like nonsense to a Greek of classical times—"to the Greeks foolishness," as St. Paul remarked—and perhaps it does to you. Certainly it is a hard mouthful for a poem to assimilate, and still harder for a play; but it is my meaning.

The poem was written about 1924, and published in 1925, in one book with "Roan Stallion" and "Tamar." Although not intended for the stage, it had, I was told, some dramatic values, and stage versions of it were made, not by me but by others. One of these was performed by students of the University of California.

Another was produced in the outdoor "Forest Theatre" of our home village, under the fog-dripping pine trees; and this time, although the cast was largely amateur, Judith Anderson took the part of Clytemnestra. Consequently the play was very successful, for its four scheduled evenings. Miss Anderson had excellent support, on the whole; but still it was a bold adventure, and a generous one, for her to take part in that chaotic and half-amateur production. She acted, of course, magnificently; so did Hilda Vaughn as Cassandra.

This was nine years ago; and Miss Anderson has constantly retained interest in the play. It was on account of this interest that she asked me to adapt the *Medea* of Euripides for the modern stage. *Medea* had a surprising success—at least to me surprising—but Miss Anderson said she regarded it as a stepping-stone toward a new production of *The Tower*.

Now, thanks to the American National Theatre and Academy, *The Tower* will be produced again, this time in New York, beginning tonight [November 26, 1950]. Judith Anderson will play Clytemnestra; and she has asked me to make the adaptation from poem to play. I have no experience of the theatre—aside from *Medea*—but I have had the advantage of Miss Anderson's advice and criticism; and in fact the adaptation has not been difficult, only ruthless; it is almost exclusively a matter of erasure. Particularly Cassandra's lamentations have been cut to the bone.

They seemed appropriate enough in the poem; but in

the theatre we are not such a patient audience as the Athenians were. Also at the very end I have introduced a piece of action—the bitter collapse of Electra—which is not in the poem, nor in the Greek stories, but here it seems to be logical and necessary. The Greeks themselves were always changing their stories, and I think we inherit the privilege.

The incestuous feeling between Electra and Orestes is another change from the Greek story. It was imagined in my poem as a symbol of our human obsession with humanity—"It is all turned inward," Orestes says—and I was interested to find it again, without that symbolic intention, when I read Eugene O'Neill's *Mourning Becomes Electra.* There was also the same rhythm of the same events—wave and counter-wave, crime and answering crime—transferred from prehistoric Greece to post-Civil War America. I have never met our great playwright, and I don't know that he ever looked at my poem, but I'd be glad to think that it may have contributed suggestions toward the making of his play. Or else that our minds worked so similarly on the Greek story.

But this is digression; I have said all that I want to say about *The Tower.* Judith Anderson's Clytemnestra will be superb—we know by experience—and I am sure the American National Theatre and Academy will do all it can for us.

S. N. BEHRMAN

What Makes Comedy High?

ONE'S RELATIVES are apt to be censorious, and a close one of mine protested to me rather explosively years ago: "When are you going to get out of that drawing room?" To that generic locale he applied an epithet not generally used in drawing rooms and which I omit here.

I believe I told him that I'd be glad to move, but that one had to live some place and I didn't have another room handy. Did he have a suggestion? He made a large gesture in the general direction of the universe. "There's a great big teeming world out there!" he said indignantly, with a baleful intimation that I was snubbing it. Somerset Maugham says somewhere—or perhaps he just said it to me—that a writer is a man who never can think of a good answer on the spot; he thinks of what he should have said when he gets back to his desk. If my critical relative will pardon the delay, I'll try to put up a ramshackle defense here for that overlong tenancy.

There is a certain confusion about three categories of plays: high comedy, drawing-room comedy, comedy of manners. In a sense every play is a comedy of manners, even if it only represents the playwright's. The category "drawing-room comedy" is arbitrary and actually meaningless; it has come to be employed as synonymous with high comedy when, essentially, it has nothing to do with it.

Any kind of play can—and has—taken place in a drawing room: farces, melodramas, spooky plays (although they generally run to libraries). Some drawing-room plays might more properly be called bathroom comedies. A high comedy can take place anywhere. *The Playboy of the Western World* is a wonderful high comedy and it doesn't remotely take place in a drawing room. Two of my favorite plays, *The Importance of Being Earnest* and *Blithe Spirit,* have most of their action in drawing rooms; they are both farces.

What makes the essence of high comedy is not the furniture of the room where the action takes place but the articulateness of the characters, the plane on which they talk, the intellectual and moral climate in which they live.

There is an idea that the characters of high comedy must be rich, well dressed, and socially elevated. This is also not necessarily true; I have done several in which the heroes were poor, badly dressed, and from the wrong side of the tracks. The immediate concerns of the characters in a high comedy may sometimes be trivial; their point of view must never be. Indeed, one of the endless sources of high comedy is seriousness of temperament and intensity of purpose in contrast with the triviality of the occasion.

Any playwright who has been up against the agony of casting plays will tell you that the actor who can play comedy is the fellow to shoot for; you will get the best performance of a serious part from an actor who can play comedy. The essence of the comic sense is awareness: awareness of the tragedy as well as of the fun of life, of the pity, the futility, the lost hopes, the striving for immortality, for permanence, for security, for love. The comic intuition gets to the heart of a human situation with a precision and a velocity unattainable in any other way. A great comic actor will do it for you with an inflection of voice as adroit as the flick of the wrist of a virtuoso fencer.

In London I saw Dame Edith Evans as Cleopatra in Shakespeare's play. She played it for high comedy. In an early scene Cleopatra is informed by Antony that his wife, Fulvia, is dead. Cleopatra's line is: "Can Fulvia die?" The Dame's reading of that line was delicious; it sent a ripple of laughter through the audience. She read it with a rising inflection of incredulity and pleasure, with a peculiar overtone of the last word which raced you through Cleopatra's mind. You heard her also saying: "Well! Evidently I have always underestimated Fulvia. I never suspected that she had the resource or the tact for a gesture like this!" Ever since then, when I see this play, I listen for the actress who plays Cleopatra to read this line; usually it comes out as a simple request for information, like: "Do you play canasta?"

Shakespeare was an excellent writer of drawing-room comedy; he did a lovely one in *Hamlet,* although he called many of his sets ramparts. The "play within a play" is a drawing-room charade. The tragedy of Hamlet—and it is well for a high comedy if it has a tragic core—is not that nearly everybody in it dies. There is nothing tragic about death; it is merely inevitable. The tragedy is that Hamlet, who really has a mind to make up, is incapable of assembling it. It is a long comedy of vacillation when decision is imperative—nicely written, of course. Hamlet suffers from a deep-seated metaphysical neurosis; Gide's remark is pertinent—that it is useful, when you are thinking about Hamlet, to remember that he attended a German university.

Some years ago I was asked to adapt an idea of Franz Werfel's which became the play, *Jacobowsky and the Colonel.* I met Elia Kazan, who was excited about the idea—and when Elia is excited he carries you along. The story was played against a background of life-and-death desperation—the flight of a French girl and a German and Polish refugee from the invading Nazis in France. I didn't go ahead with it till I got the notion of making the German refugee, Jacobowsky, a humorous and cultivated man, nurtured in the humanities; the Pole, a noble, elegant, humorless, and literal man, nurtured in the tradition of military glory.

The French girl they both love finds that she can laugh with Jacobowsky; this laughter drives the Pole crazy. He cannot break the magic circle of this laughter; he finds it more difficult than storming a redoubt. The play was, therefore, high comedy, though there were sinister Nazis and hairbreadth escapes in it.

It is amusing to read in the papers of the Russians' desperation over their comedic output and their dissatisfaction with their machines for impressing joy. How true to type the dictatorships run! It is "Kraft durch Freude" over again. The fanatics know dimly that there might be something to laugh at hovering around somewhere if they could only find it. But they are really afraid to find it because of their terror that it might shatter some of their basic assumptions. For laughter is the most humanizing—as well as the most critical—agency in the world.

The ability to laugh at its own pretensions and shortcomings is the true mark of the civilized nation, as it is of the civilized man. It will take the Russians a thousand years —if they're snappy—to develop anybody like Gilbert and Sullivan. When Gilbert made fun of the House of Lords and threatened its members with the disaster of "competitive examination" he did them in, long before Asquith got around to it.

I know that the press agent for my new play at the Coronet Theatre will be unhappy if I don't mention *Jane,* and it is a primary function of the playwright to keep the press agent in amiable spirits. Maugham's short story, on which the play is based, tells about an elderly frump from Liverpool who marries a very young and very attractive man. Miss Theresa Helburn of the Theatre Guild wished me to adapt it. Mr. Maugham, who is one of the canniest of men, has sold the film rights to everything he has ever written—he has recently even been selling the rights to his fascinating personality; but he never sold the film rights to *Jane,* although it is over thirty years old, because he felt that it would one day make a play.

Although he is a brilliant playwright, he did not want to dramatize it himself because he has long since quit the theatre, which is perhaps an even profounder demonstration of his canniness. It looked to me like an attractive job but it was very hard to do. The theatre is the most naked of mediums; it is a two-and-a-half-hour close-up, and questions which Maugham never had to answer—nor even to raise—in the compass of a short story, pop up uncomfortably when you come to write a play. Why does a sensible woman like Jane marry a man so much younger? Maugham describes her as witty and as making a sensation by always telling the truth. Nice work if you can get it! Also, and this is the nub, instead of the young man's eventually leaving Jane, as everyone predicts, Jane leaves the young man. This was a puzzler. Why? I gave this as much thought as Newton and Satan gave the apple—with somewhat less epochal results. One line gave the play to me and the answer. When Gilbert asks Jane why she is leaving him, she says: "Because you are too old for me." This line was, originally, the curtain of Act Two, the climax of the play. In the prolonged neurasthenic hypochondria which constitutes a tryout tour, I allowed this line to be shifted to Act Three. The point I wanted to make in the play is that youth is a question of vitality, generosity, warmth, and general sympathy in point of view. A stuffed shirt may be old at twenty. Jane is alive and vital and will be young at eighty.

Probably, after he reads this, my critical relative will say what he said long before: "When are you going to get ***," etc. I will still have to answer: "Probably never." Nor do I feel cramped. When the Captains and the Kings depart, their stories will be told in drawing rooms, even if they are merely living rooms or libraries or studies or just dens.

ARCHIBALD MacLEISH

The Poet as Playwright

1

ONE WOULD feel happier about the future of poetry on the stage were it not for the defensiveness of those who proclaim it. Poetry had used the theatre and the theatre had used poetry for thousands of years before prose took over but our contemporaries—even the best of them, even Mr. Eliot—go on as though the play in verse still required justification. "No play," said Mr. Eliot at Harvard four years ago, "should be written in verse for which prose is *dramatically* adequate." That judgment might have been expected from a Broadway critic, most of whom would put the period after the word "verse," but it has a defunctive sound in the mouth of the most successful dramatic poet of our generation. If Mr. Eliot admits it, then prose is indeed the appropriate language for the modern stage and the poet can be welcomed only on those rare occasions when prose has already failed.

And yet dramatic poetry has flourished under many and various conditions in the past and ours is an age in which it might very conceivably be expected to flourish again. When an age is an age of actions as ours is, and when men live in confusion and die in ignorance for lack of that very perception of the meaning of their acts which poetry on the stage has given in other times and places, and which prose has yet to give in like measure or with a comparable intensity, a renewal of dramatic poetry would

---

First published in *The Atlantic Monthly*, CVC (February, 1955), 49–52, and reprinted here with the permission of Archibald MacLeish.

seem possible. We go back willingly enough in our generation to those mirrors of human meaning which poetic
drama has provided to earlier men: we go back to *Julius
Caesar* and to *Macbeth* and above all to *Hamlet*. Why then
do we advise the playwrights of our own time, who know
its temper and who live with its persistent questions, to
write in prose wherever prose will serve?

An obvious explanation would be that ours is an "unpoetic" generation. We hear it said often enough and every
now and again we run across a writer who does his best,
consciously or unconsciously, to prove it true. But the fact
is, first, that we aren't "unpoetic," and, second, that it
would not explain our attitude toward poetry on the stage
if we were, and, finally, that the theory in any case would
scarcely account for Mr. Eliot, who is so far from being
"unpoetic" that he is one of the principal poets now alive.
Books of poetry do not sell by the thousands of copies per
day as some of Byron's did, but they are read—Yeats, for
example, and Rilke's *Duino Elegies*—far more seriously
and to far greater purpose. The reading of poetry for
"pleasure" may have gone out with the first Romantics, and
its passing may very properly be regretted, but the reading
of poetry for understanding has more than taken its place.
And not among the specialists alone. Upwards of five thousand people sat in a raw wind in the Public Garden in
Boston on a June evening last year to listen to Robert
Frost; and Boston, as those who read its newspapers are
aware, is no longer the city of the Brahmins.

No, something more than an imaginary aversion to poetry is involved in our skittishness about verse in the theatre, and Mr. Eliot's dictum indicates pretty clearly, I
think, what it is. The trouble lies not in our feeling about
poetry but in our feeling about the theatre. To say that
no play should be written in verse for which prose is dramatically adequate is to say something, not about verse,
but about the nature of a play, or rather about the conception of a play which is current at this particular time
and place. Mr. Eliot is not saying that prose is better than
verse for most purposes. Mr. Eliot is saying that a play, as
we conceive of it (for he is not offering his advice to

Aeschylus or Racine), is something which, by its nature, demands prose wherever prose will serve.

Before we ask the appropriate question, why? there is an incidental assumption underlying all this, as it underlies so much similar talk, which must be examined. It is an assumption which comes oddly from Mr. Eliot. I refer to the implicit idea that the choice of verse or prose is a free choice which a playwright may make on rational or at least technical grounds. Few poets—Yeats on occasion and a very few others—have been tempted to write plays in prose and no prose writers, with Mr. Maxwell Anderson as the distinguished exception to prove the rule, have been tempted to write plays in verse. What is more likely to happen is what seems to have happened to Mr. Eliot himself: a poet wishing to write for the stage undertakes to write *as poet* and makes it his task to teach himself how, as poet, to make his poetry dramatic. Or a prose writer, similarly seduced, labors to adapt his prose to his new medium without a thought to the possibility that he might turn himself into a poet first. The figure of the playwright with a plot in mind, debating with himself whether to write it out in verse or prose, is thus a figure made of straw. In most cases the decision will have been made in advance, and in any case the play itself will have at least as much to say about the result as the playwright or the critic who advises him. But this latter is a dark subject to which we must return.

2

The question to be answered first is the question Mr. Eliot poses. Why should prose take precedence in the contemporary theatre? Mr. Eliot explains with his usual lucidity and patience. The difference between prose and verse on the stage is not that one is natural and the other artificial: both are artificial. The difference is that theatre audiences, either because they make no distinction between the talk they hear at home and the talk they hear in a prose dialogue, or because they are able to ignore the distinction when they do notice it, *think* of prose on the stage as natural whereas poetry on the stage, being noticeably different from the talk at home, *seems* to them artificial. Audiences, in other words, are conscious of the poetry as poetry but not conscious of the prose as prose. And this consciousness of the poetry as poetry is a dramatic liability, whether the audience likes the poetry or dislikes it, for it gets in the way of the dramatic action. Which seems to mean that it gets in the way of the audience's acceptance of the lifelikeness of the dramatic action.

We are thus given the measure of the dramatic superiority of prose to verse. The measure is the audience's willingness to accept what it hears as "true to life." The dramatic demands of the contemporary stage are the demands imposed by an audience which wishes to receive a particular illusion from the actions it witnesses and the words it hears: the illusion that it is seeing and hearing *life the way it is.* It is this measure, Mr. Eliot is saying, which determines the superiority of prose for most plays. And it is this measure also which determines, for Mr. Eliot, the superiority of verse on those occasions when prose is inadequate and verse should take its place. He puts it this way: ". . . beyond the namable, classifiable emotions and motives of our conscious life when directed towards action—the part of life which prose drama is wholly adequate to express—there is a fringe of indefinite extent, of feelings which we can only detect, so to speak, out of the corner of the eye and can never completely focus. . . . This peculiar range of sensibility can be expressed by dramatic poetry, at its moments of greatest intensity."

That there is such a range of sensibility, a range which can only be expressed by that particular organization of language which poetry is—that organization which combines, as Coleridge saw, an unusual degree of order with an unusual degree of freedom from order—all readers of poetry will acknowledge. Only those who, through ignorance of poetry, are ignorant of the existence of the sensibility it expresses will question Mr. Eliot's statement. But what is important here is not the truth of the statement but the use to which it is being put. Poetry, Mr. Eliot says, is permissible on the stage in dealing with actions which impinge on this "fringe of feeling" not merely because poetry is capable of the expression of these feelings whereas prose is not, but because, *when such feelings are involved, the theatre audience will accept poetry as "true to life."* Mr. Eliot is explicit about it. The audience, he says, should find "at the moment of awareness that it is hearing poetry, that it is saying to itself: '*I* could talk in poetry too!'"

Both the rule and the exception, therefore, are justified on the same ground—the audience's acceptance of the language in either case as true to life or lifelike. What is involved, in other words, is a preconception of the nature of the illusion the modern stage is expected to create. If you take the position that the language of the theatre should be the language which audiences regard as most like actual talk, or, in the exceptional case, as most like the language they themselves would use under the emotional circumstances, you are assuming that the illusion the contemporary theatre exists to create is the illusion of actuality.

Now there is, of course, wide support for this conception of the demands of contemporary audiences. In that part of our theatre to which the invidious, and not infrequently envious, adjective "commercial" is applied, the illusion of the actual is the standard target. Everything is made as much like itself as possible and the appetite which is satisfied is the appetite the newspapers arouse. But because the illusion of the actual is the illusion served by the contemporary theatre in its most successful forms it does not necessarily follow that the illusion of the actual is the only illusion the stage can provide or our generation is capable of accepting. Nor does it follow that a modern defense of poetry on the stage must ground itself on that restricted foundation.

I have nothing but admiration for Mr. Eliot's gallant purpose to reconquer a place on the contemporary stage for poetry by bringing poetry into overt competition, as he phrases it, with prose. Prose has had the stage pretty much to itself for the past hundred years largely because poetry has refused to compete with it, preferring instead to retire to a private literary world of its own where, to all dramatic intents and purposes, it has palely perished. Plays have been written in verse for generations and no one has cared, not even the versifiers—least of all, indeed, the versifiers. If there is one body of printed matter to which the contemporary poet does not wish to return, it is to the body—carcass rather—of double-columned pages produced in the name of drama by the poets of the nineteenth century; Mr. Eliot is the first poet of distinction and stature to attempt to invade the public stage *as public stage* in a very long time, Yeats alone excepted.

But greatly as one must admire Mr. Eliot's good sense and gallantry, one must question, notwithstanding, the strategy he has adopted. Granted that the stage is a battlefield where a play must fight for its life in competition with other plays and under conditions established by the sensibility of the audience, whatever the audience of the moment may be, it does not inevitably follow that the field can be won only by emulating the contemporary masters and accepting the dramatic illusion they have so successfully exploited.

There are other illusions within the capacity of the stage and there are other illusions within the reach of the human heart. There is, for one example, the illusion—very different from the illusion of the actual—of the real. Virginia Woolf's casual suggestion in her *Diary* that the test of the novel is its power to "enhance one's vision of life" defines the difference. The illusion of the real is the illusion, whether in the novel or on the stage, not that this is the *actual* man, true to life, but that this is the man *himself:* not that this action is an action *like* life but that this action *is* life—what life really is. It is an illusion which the stage knows well and has known since its beginnings. The plot of *Oedipus* with its long-forgotten murder and its sudden rush of discoveries is as improbable in any actual terms as a plot could be, but the illusion *Oedipus* creates is an illusion of the revelation of the web of human fate which men have accepted as a perception of the reality of their lives for thousands of years. Shakespeare's *Tempest* is as remote from actuality as Prospero's island but its metaphor is a metaphor which tells us more about ourselves than any newspaper has ever told us. Yeats's *Purgatory* has no prototype in actuality but it casts its shadow in the country where things *are*.

Moreover, as these examples suggest, the illusion of the real is an illusion which dramatic poetry can pursue at least as well as dramatic prose. The illusion of the real is indeed the principal business of poetry. It is to know our own reality as living, feeling beings that poetry is written and that poetry is read. And the theatre does not differ from the printed page in this regard. The power of Shakespeare's finest plays to penetrate the human mystery is a power given them in great part by their poetry, as every listening audience knows.

3

Why then should a defense of poetry on the modern stage be written on the assumption that the sole illusion permissible to the stage is the illusion of the actual? The answer, in Mr. Eliot's case, is apparently that modern audiences will accept nothing else—that modern audiences wish to regard the stage not as a stage for art but as a peephole into actuality and that the playwright must accept that fact, shaping his language to meet the public expectation. An actual couple in an actual bar would not address each other in verses and therefore this couple on the stage, committed by their observers to an actuality as strict as that of a newspaper column, must not speak in verses either. To introduce verse would be to ask the audience to accept a dramatic convention and modern audiences detest dramatic conventions.

Well, they may think they do but the fact is, of course, that no convention could conceivably be more conventional than the convention of the modern peephole theatre by which some hundreds of human beings sit solidly on rows of soft substantial seats agreeing to pretend the man and woman on the stage are quite alone and no one else is there. An audience which will accept the convention of its own absence from the theatre where it sits will accept anything. I doubt, however, that the question really is one of conventions. I should guess that it was a question, rather, of the immutability of that attitude of modern audiences to which Mr. Eliot attaches such overriding importance.

There is no question, of course, but that the expectation

of the audience is a limiting factor so far as the playwright is concerned. Does it, however, follow that that expectation is an immutable and fixed condition about which the playwright can do nothing? Do audiences accept the verse of Shakespeare's plays because they have been taught in school they should, or do they accept it because the expectations the plays arouse in them are expectations with which the verse accords? I should guess, the latter. I should guess that what enables Shakespeare's people to speak poetry even to a modern audience is the fact that it is poetry the audience expects and, furthermore, that that expectation is one the play itself creates. The plays do not offer to present the world of actuality. They are, quite frankly, plays—works of art. Which is to say that they are, like all works of art, worlds complete in themselves: worlds in which the speaking of verse is accepted as naturally as the colors of a picture. Because *Hamlet* offers, not a glimpse of the private life of a Danish court, but a perception of the nature of the human heart, the language of poetry seems not inappropriate to it, even in ears where poetry is seldom heard.

But if this is true of Shakespeare, why may it not be true for lesser men? Why may not the justification of verse on the stage, even in a time like ours, be found in the play itself? Mr. Eliot insists, and rightly I think, that there are no "poetic subjects": no subjects for plays which, by their nature, call for verse. A poetic drama may be made out of any experience of which men are capable, no matter how ordinary or, as the word goes, prosaic. But because there are no poetic subjects—no inherently poetic actions—it does not follow that there are no poetic *organizations of action*—no organizations of action on the stage which require poetry for their realization. An action so organized as to reveal not only its dramatic character, but its human significance, demands much of its language. And it is when the expressive demands are heaviest that prose gives way. Prose is a magnificent instrument of communication, but when understanding must be achieved, not by the mind but by the emotions as well, by the senses, by the whole being, poetry which reaches the mind through the senses and the emotions, which calls the whole being into play, goes on alone. There is no equivalent in prose for the lyric poem for the self-evident reason that it is precisely what distinguishes poetry from prose that makes the lyric poem— the ultimate margin.

The fundamental justification for poetry on the stage, in other words, is not the one given by Mr. Eliot. It is not that the audience finds itself feeling, at a given moment of emotional intensification, "*I* could talk in poetry too!" The fundamental justification lies in the play itself, in the illusion the play undertakes to create, in the kind of understanding the play communicates. To go far one must go by art. To go farthest one must use art in its ultimate resource. The question at that point is no longer a question of the naturalness of the language spoken on the stage. The only question there is a question of the language's effectiveness. An audience does not accept the poetry of the end of *Antony and Cleopatra* because "*I* could talk in poetry too!" but because there are no other words than these to say what is being said.

But the point is not that Mr. Eliot's theory and example are open to question. Mr. Eliot's great reputation is secure. The point is that the conception of poetry on the stage as a mere means of expression, alternative to prose, the use of which is justified only in the case of certain inexplicable feelings, distracts attention from the true problem of the modern dramatic poet. The true problem is the problem of the poetic organization of action in such a time as ours. To regain the stage in its own character, not as a mere emulation of prose, poetry must find its own poetic way to the mastery the stage demands—the mastery of action. What poetry in English has lost is not expressive skill. The craftsmanship of the art of verse is at a high point in this country and in England. What poetry has lost is the power to imitate an action. It has become inward and reflective to such a point that the great metaphors of action, which are the true figures of the poetic stage, are beyond its competence. Until it can people the stage again with actions which are at once poetry *and* drama, poetic drama will not exist.

That end will not be achieved by adopting for poetry the illusion of the actual. The poet who adopts the illusion of the actual can bring poetry to the stage only by half persuading his audience that it is prose they are attending: the better he succeeds as playwright the less he will succeed as poet. Poetry will return to the stage, not when its presence is concealed, but when the audience is brought to expect it and, expecting it, to need it. That expectation only the illusion of the real can create. The poet as playwright must so manage his actions and his language as to produce the illusion that the world of his play is a world in which reality may itself appear, as the God may come to the bridge in one of the ancient no plays of Japan.

ELMER RICE

American Theatre and the Human Spirit

IT WAS, I believe, Anatole France who defined criticism as the adventures of a soul among masterpieces. But most critics necessarily function upon a far less exalted plane. Not only is there, at any given moment, a scarcity of masterpieces, but the number of souls capable of high adventure is equally rare. The practitioner of the arts who attempts to evaluate the work of his contemporaries embarks upon a dubious undertaking. If he is hypocritical or consciously tactful, he will extravagantly overpraise his fellow artists (particularly if they happen to be his personal friends); if he is spiteful or envious, he will be unfairly disparaging. But even if he tries to be impersonal or impartial, unconscious influences will color his judgment. Either he will elevate his co-workers and thus, by association, become a member of a glorious company; or else, painfully aware of his shortcomings, he will find solace in bringing others down to his own level.

For these reasons, if for no other, I shall in this discussion of the contemporary drama in America refrain from commenting upon individual writers or their works, but shall limit myself to an attempt to discover what ideological, cultural, and psychological trends are discernible in the American theatre of today. And though I speak of the American theatre I believe that its essential qualities are more or less characteristic of the theatre of the whole Western world.

To begin with, we must remind ourselves that the artist, and particularly the dramatist, does not exist in a vacuum.

First published in *Saturday Review* of December 17, 1955, and reprinted here with the permission of Elmer Rice.

He is a product of his times, and is most effective and significant when he expresses and reflects the currents of
thought and of feeling that prevail in the society in which
he lives. I say particularly the dramatist, for the drama is
primarily a mass art. It addresses itself to the crowd rather
than to the individual. And we all know that the responses
of the crowd are more conservative, more emotional, less
differentiated, than are those of the individuals who compose it. Furthermore, the fluid and kinetic nature of the
drama makes it imperative that apprehension be swift and
unmistakable. There is no time for reflection, no time to
turn back the page, to view the image from more than one
angle, to examine the texture of the material. What is not
instantly grasped is forever lost. Hence, the dramatist, more
than any other artist, must express himself in terms of the
tempo and the outlook of his era. His rôle is not that of
the thinker, the innovator, the discoverer, but, at his best,
that of a catalytic agent, who fuses and vivifies what is
already deeply believed or unconsciously felt by his audience. His work projects only what is already discernible:
he is the mirror of his times.

All plays deal with the nature of man, and with his relationship to his fellow men, and to the material and
spiritual universe. If we look swiftly at three great periods
of world drama, we see, at once, how man's concept of
himself is portrayed by the dramatist. To the Greeks man
was an exalted, even a semi-divine being, the chief preoccupation of the gods on Olympus, and often on extremely
intimate terms with them. His life's course was determined
by inevitable destiny and inexorable moral laws. When the
fallible protagonist of the Greek play came to his tragic
end it was not defeat that was signalized, but rather the
affirmation and vindication of universal principles of human behavior.

In Elizabethan times the gods were less dominant, but
the world was still anthropocentric; it was still possible for
man to believe that there was a divinity that shaped his
ends. The Renaissance had awakened the Western world
from the long sleep of the Middle Ages. It was a period of
adventure and of discovery: the classics of antiquity and
the New World beyond the seas. Man was flexing his

muscles and proclaiming himself monarch of all he surveyed. His authority may have been recognized as brief, but he was still man, proud man. It has always seemed significant to me that *Hamlet* does not end with the heaping up of corpses at the court of Elsinore, but is carried on a beat farther to the triumphal entry of Fortinbras. The hero dies, but the life-cycle and the continuity of law and order are unbroken. The eloquence, the passion, the reckless splendor that sparkle and thunder through the Elizabethan drama are but expressions of the sanguine exuberance that characterized that dazzling era.

By the middle of the nineteenth century, however, revolutionary political events and scientific theories had drastically altered man's conception of himself and of his relation to the universe. As his horizons widened, his own stature shrank correspondingly. The Industrial Revolution had destroyed the last vestiges of the feudal system. Political science, in theory at least, had reduced all men to a common level of equality. Evolutionary science had formulated the disconcerting hypothesis that man, far from being the unique product of a special creation, is merely a remote and rather complicated descendant of the amoeba. In terms of the dramatic art it was no longer possible to picture him as a godlike creature, whose personal destiny was a matter of cosmic importance. It was possible, however, to substitute for divine justice the somewhat less exalted concept of social justice. The heroes of Ibsen and his followers went forth to battle against the hypocrisies, falsehoods, and inequities of an outmoded social order. They bore aloft the banner of the ideal. They failed because they were imperfect, or because the forces arrayed against them were too powerful; but they did not despair. I am oversimplifying, of course; but I think it can be fairly said that even the pessimism of the late nineteenth century sprang from anger and impatience with man's mistakes and follies rather than from lack of faith in his possibilities.

The turn of the century brought with it the new psychology. I think it is no exaggeration to say that the theories of Freud have altered man's conception of himself as radically as did those of Darwin and of Marx. We learned from him that our conscious life is merely the surface manifestation of a complex of impulses that lies hidden in the dark and perilous waters of the unconscious. We are all, it seems, ridden by fears and anxieties, tortured by feelings of guilt and of inferiority, remorselessly driven by morbid compulsions. We spend our lives in a frantic effort to compensate for our inadequacies and frustrations. Actions that once seemed noble now appear to be merely protective coloration for destructive or shameful desires. Moral values are illusory: a mask for the true amorality of our natures. Basically we are all insecure and, to make matters worse, our insecurity more often than not springs from infantile or even prenatal misadventures, beyond awareness or the range of memory.

Meanwhile the outer world has been blasted by two devastating wars; the threat of a third, even more devastating, hangs over us. Whether these catastrophes are the product of our fears and frustrations or have merely served to aggravate them is irrelevant here. I am trying to say only that there is an increasing emphasis upon the mental derangements that beset humanity. The dislocations of war have robbed millions of psychic, as well as of physical, security. The crime rate mounts steadily. The ever-increasing incidence of divorce is evidence not only of the inability of people to make emotional adjustments but of the disruption of the normal emotional patterns of countless children. In the United States more than half the hospital beds are occupied by mental patients, and there is an incessant demand for increased facilities. And, of course, those requiring hospitalization are only a fraction of the mentally disturbed. Recourse to psychiatric therapy is no longer a luxurious pastime for the wealthy or the idle; it has become for many an indispensable requisite. People now speak of "my analyst" as they speak of "my dentist" or "my tailor." A recent comic drawing in *The New Yorker* showed a psychoanalyst's office displaying a sign which read: "Six couches; no waiting."

What was fifty years ago an esoteric scientific theory has seeped down to the popular level. It permeates our medical institutions and our law-courts; our prisons and our schools. The major part of American commercial advertising is deliberately and cynically designed to play upon the emotions of fear, shame, anxiety, and envy. In ever-increasing numbers, the presses pour forth scientific and pseudo-scientific treatises that discuss and interpret our social and personal problems in terms of psychic dislocations, emotional maladjustments, and escape mechanisms.

It is not surprising, therefore, to find in the work of our playwrights—those weathervanes of the popular climate—unmistakable indications of which way the wind is blowing. The prevailing tone is not so much pessimism as disillusionment, despair, and even disgust. T. S. Eliot, Nobel Prize winner and the most influential contemporary poet —as well as a brilliant playwright—has summed it up in these words: "This is the way the world ends; not with a bang, but a whimper." (Though in view of the progress of atomic science it may be a bang, after all.)

At any rate, the tragic hero, as protagonist, has almost ceased to exist. The figure of noble stature charged with high destiny, impelled by profound passions, has become obsolete. The heroes of the drama of today, if they can be called heroes, are bewildered creatures, floundering in a morass of self-delusion, self-pity, and frustration; drugging themselves with wishful fantasies; destroying those closest to them with a surfeit or dearth of love.

Recently there has appeared a volume by W. David Sievers, an American university professor, provocatively entitled *Freud on Broadway*. In this closely-printed book of 500 pages the author examines the works of American playwrights during the last three or four decades, in the light of psychoanalytic theory. While some of his interpretations are certainly a little strained, there can be no doubt that the general conclusions of his survey are both convincing and startling. Almost without exception every contemporary playwright reveals in his work the strong influence of the new approach to human relationships and human behavior. Like Molière's hero who discovered to his astonishment that he had been speaking prose all his life, the amazed playwright may learn from these pages that he has been consistently expounding the new psychology.

Though it is not my intention to cite the work of individual dramatists, a few general observations will, I hope, illustrate my brief diagnosis of the present state of the drama. It is remarkable, for example, that the contemporary drama fails almost entirely to deal with the problems of adults. By adults, of course, I do not mean merely persons who have attained their legal majority, but integrated individuals who are emotionally secure and who are capable of conducting their lives in a healthful and constructive manner. Psychiatric therapy casts doubts upon the existence of such individuals; but if they do exist they rarely find their way into the plays of today. Instead, our drama deals almost exclusively with the problems of children and of adolescents—actual or arrested. This is not surprising, for the news has spread that we are not responsible for what we are or do, but that all our shortcomings, maladjustments, and failures can be traced back to our childhood environment, and more particularly to the mistakes and inadequacies of those who presided over our formative years. The twentieth century has been called the century of the child, and with some justice, for not only is there a new and, on the whole, salutary interest in the well-being of children, but adults tend more and more to identify themselves with their children or, by taking refuge in childhood memories, to escape from or find answers to the problems of the present.

For many years now the chief villains of the drama have been the possessive mother and the dominating father. And the hero, if not actually a child or an adolescent, is an adult who is still chained to his past, or whose appetites and desires have been curbed, distorted, or perverted. The recurrent themes of our plays are loneliness, rebellion against parental authority, incest-longings, emotional starvation, escape mechanisms, juvenile delinquency, crimes of violence, homosexuality, terror fantasies, sadism, and schizophrenia.

I am aware that I have painted a gloomy picture, but I have not done so with the intention of disparaging or castigating the playwrights of today. They, like the players, are but the brief and abstract chroniclers of the times. Their work, as I have said, merely epitomizes the contemporary attitude toward life. On the artistic side of the dramatic art America need not be ashamed of itself. We have many sensitive, forceful playwrights whose work displays great technical skill and literary excellence. In my forty years in the American theatre I have seen a constant rise in the general level of dramatic writing. In the face of increasingly difficult economic conditions and severe competition from the media of mass entertainment the theatre manages to survive—as it always has, and always will, for nothing equals it as an apparatus for the projection of man's fantasies.

If, at present, the drama is at a lower spiritual and intellectual level than we would wish it to be it is because we live in a time of anti-intellectualism and spiritual negation. We have taken the human mechanism apart in an effort to find out why it does not tick, but we have not yet discovered the formula for reassembling it so that its triumphant carillon may ring out to heaven. In splitting the atom and splitting the ego we have unleashed forces that may destroy us, unless we find a synthesis that will employ atomic energy for peaceful uses, and psychic energy for restoring to man a belief in his own dignity and creative potentialities. If that happy time ever comes, I think that the dramatists of the world, including those of America, will know how to celebrate the renascence of the human spirit.

THORNTON WILDER

A Platform and a Passion or Two

TOWARD the end of the twenties I began to lose pleasure in going to the theatre. I ceased to believe in the stories I saw presented there. When I did go it was to admire some secondary aspect of the play, the work of a great actor or director or designer. Yet at the same time the conviction was growing in me that the theatre was the greatest of all the arts. I felt that something had gone wrong with it in my time and that it was fulfilling only a small part of its potentialities. I was filled with admiration for presentations of classical works by Max Reinhardt and Louis Jouvet and the Old Vic, as I was by the best plays of my own time, like *Desire Under the Elms* and *The Front Page;* but at heart I didn't believe a word of them. I was like a schoolmaster grading a paper; to each of these offerings I gave an A+, but the condition of mind of one grading a paper is not that of one being overwhelmed by an artistic creation. The response we make when we "believe" a work of the imagination is that of saying: "This is the way things are. I have always known it without being fully aware that I knew it. Now in the presence of this play or novel or poem (or picture or piece of music) I know that I know it." It is this form of knowledge which Plato called "recollection." We have all murdered, in thought; and been murdered. We have all seen the ridiculous in estimable persons and in ourselves. We have all known terror as well as enchantment. Imaginative literature has nothing to say to those who do not recognize—who cannot be *reminded*—of such conditions. Of all the arts the theatre is best endowed to awaken this recollection within us—to believe is to say "yes"; but in the theatres of my time I did not feel myself prompted to any such grateful and self-forgetting acquiescence.

This dissatisfaction worried me. I was not ready to condemn myself as blasé and overfastidious, for I knew that I was still capable of belief. I believed every word of *Ulysses* and of Proust and of *The Magic Mountain,* as I did of hundreds of plays when I read them. It was on the stage that imaginative narration became false. Finally, my dissatisfaction passed into resentment. I began to feel that the theatre was not only inadequate, it was evasive; it did not wish to draw upon its deeper potentialities. I found the word for it: it aimed to be *soothing.* The tragic had no heat; the comic had no bite; the social criticism failed to indict us with responsibility. I began to search for the point where the theatre had run off the track, where it had chosen—and been permitted—to become a minor art and an inconsequential diversion.

The trouble began in the nineteenth century and was connected with the rise of the middle classes—they wanted their theatre soothing. There's nothing wrong with the middle classes in themselves. We know that now. The United States and Scandinavia and Germany are middle-class countries, so completely so that they have lost the very memory of their once despised and ludicrous inferiority (they had been inferior not only to the aristocracy but, in human dignity, to the peasantry). When a middle class is new, however, there is much that is wrong with it. When it is emerging from under the shadow of an aristocracy, from the myth and prestige of those well-born Higher-ups, it is alternately insecure and aggressively complacent. It must find its justification and reassurance in making money and displaying it. To this day, members of the middle classes in England, France, and Italy feel themselves to be a little ridiculous and humiliated. The prestige of aristocracies is based upon a dreary untruth that moral superiority and the qualifications for leadership are transmittable through the chromosomes, and the secondary lie, that the environment afforded by privilege and leisure tends to nurture the flowers of the spirit. An aristocracy, defending and fostering its lie, extracts from the arts only such elements as can further its interests, the aroma and not the sap, the grace and not the trenchancy. Equally harmful to culture is the newly arrived middle class. In the English-speaking world the middle classes came into power early in the nineteenth century and gained control over the theatre. They were pious, law-abiding, and industrious. They were assured of eternal life in the next world and, in this, they were squarely seated on Property and the privileges that accompany it. They were attended by devoted servants who knew their place. They were benevolent within certain limits, but chose to ignore wide tracts of injustice and stupidity in the world about them; and they shrank from contemplating those elements within themselves that were ridiculous, shallow, and harmful. They distrusted the passions and tried to deny them. Their questions about the nature of life seemed to be sufficiently answered by the demonstration of financial status and by conformity to some clearly established rules of decorum. These were precarious positions; abysses yawned on either side. The air was loud with questions that must not be asked. These audiences fashioned a theatre which could not disturb them. They thronged to melodrama (which deals with tragic possibilities in such a way that you know from the beginning that all will end happily) and to sentimental drama (which accords a total license to the supposition that the wish is father to the thought) and to comedies in which the characters were so represented that they always resembled someone else and not oneself. Between the plays that Sheridan wrote in his twenties and the first works of Wilde and Shaw there was no play of even moderate interest written in the English language. (Unless you happen to admire and except Shelley's *The Cenci.*) These audiences, however, also thronged to Shakespeare. How did they shield themselves against his probing? How did they smother the theatre—and with such effect that it smothers us still? The box set was already there, the curtain, the proscenium, but not taken "seriously"—it was a convenience in view of the weather in northern countries. They took it seriously and emphasized and enhanced everything that thus removed, cut off, and boxed the action; they increasingly shut the play up into a museum showcase.

Let us examine why the box-set stage stifles the life in drama and why and how it militates against belief.

Every action which has ever taken place—every thought, every emotion—has taken place only once, at one moment in time and place. "I love you," "I rejoice," "I suffer," have been said and felt many billions of times, and never twice the same. Every person who has ever lived has lived an unbroken succession of unique occasions. Yet the more one is aware of this individuality in experience (innumerable! innumerable!) the more one becomes attentive to what these disparate moments have in common, to repetitive patterns. As an artist (or listener or beholder) which "truth" do you prefer—that of the isolated occasion, or that which includes and resumes the innumerable? Which truth is more worth telling? Every age differs in this. Is the Venus de Milo "one woman"? Is the play *Macbeth* the story of "one destiny"? The theatre is admirably fitted to tell both truths. It has one foot planted firmly in the particular, since each actor before us (even when he wears a mask!) is indubitably a living breathing "one"; yet it tends and strains to exhibit a general truth since its relation to a specific "realistic" truth is confused and undermined by the fact that it is an accumulation of untruths, pretenses, and fiction. The novel is pre-eminently the vehicle of the unique occasion, the theatre of the generalized one. It is through the theatre's power to raise the exhibited individual action into the realm of idea and type and universal that it is able to evoke our belief. But power is precisely what those nineteenth-century audiences did not —dared not—confront. They tamed it and drew its teeth; squeezed it into that removed showcase. They loaded the stage with specific objects, because every concrete object on the stage fixes and narrows the action to one moment in time and place. (Have you ever noticed that in the plays of Shakespeare no one—except occasionally a ruler —ever sits down? There were not even chairs on the English or Spanish stages in the time of Elizabeth I.) So it was by a jugglery with time that the middle classes devitalized the theatre. When you emphasize *place* in the theatre, you drag down and limit and harness time to it. You thrust the action back into past time, whereas it is precisely the glory of the stage that it is always "now" there. Under such production methods the characters are all dead before the action starts. You don't have to pay deeply from your heart's participation. No great age in the theatre ever attempted to capture the audiences' belief through this kind of specification and localization. I became dissatisfied with the theatre because I was unable to lend credence to such childish attempts to be "real."

I began writing one-act plays that tried to capture not verisimilitude but reality. In *The Happy Journey to Trenton and Camden* four kitchen chairs represent an automobile and a family travels seventy miles in twenty minutes. Ninety years go by in *The Long Christmas Dinner*. In *Pullman Car Hiawatha* some more plain chairs serve as berths and we hear the very vital statistics of the towns and fields that passengers are traversing; we hear their thoughts; we even hear the planets over their heads. In Chinese drama a character, by straddling a stick, conveys to us that he is on horseback. In almost every no play of the Japanese an actor makes a tour of the stage and we know that he is making a long journey. Think of the ubiquity that Shakespeare's stage afforded for the battle scenes at the close of *Julius Caesar* and *Antony and Cleopatra*. As we see them today what a cutting and hacking of the text takes place—what condescension, what contempt for his dramaturgy.

Our Town is not offered as a picture of life in a New Hampshire village; or as a speculation about the conditions of life after death (that element I merely took from Dante's *Purgatory*). It is an attempt to find a value above all price for the smallest events in our daily life. I have made the claim as preposterous as possible, for I have set the village against the largest dimensions of time and place. The recurrent words in this play (few have noticed it) are "hundreds," "thousands," and "millions." Emily's joys and griefs, her algebra lessons and her birthday presents—what are they when we consider all the billions of girls who have lived, who are living, and who will live? Each individual's assertion to an absolute reality can only be inner, very inner. And here the method of staging finds its justification —in the first two acts there are at least a few chairs and tables; but when she revisits the earth and the kitchen to which she descended on her twelfth birthday, the very chairs and table are gone. Our claim, our hope, our despair are in the mind—not in things, not in "scenery." Molière said that for the theatre all he needed was a platform and a passion or two. The climax of this play needs only five square feet of boarding and the passion to know what life means to us.

The Matchmaker is an only slightly modified version of *The Merchant of Yonkers,* which I wrote in the year after I had written *Our Town.* One way to shake off the nonsense of the nineteenth-century staging is to make fun of it. This play parodies the stock-company plays that I used to see at Ye Liberty Theatre, Oakland, California, when I was a boy. I have already read small theses in German comparing it with the great Austrian original on which it is based. The scholars are very bewildered. There is most of the plot (except that our friend Dolly Levi is not in Nestroy's play); there are some of the tags; but it's all "about" quite different matters. My play is about the aspirations of the young (and not only of the young) for a fuller, freer participation in life. Imagine an Austrian pharmacist going to the shelf to draw from a bottle which he knows to contain a stinging corrosive liquid, guaranteed to remove warts and wens; and imagine his surprise when he discovers that it has been filled overnight with very American birch-bark beer.

The Skin of Our Teeth begins, also, by making fun of old-fashioned playwriting; but the audience soon perceives that he is seeing "two times at once." The Antrobus family is living both in prehistoric times and in a New Jersey commuter's suburb today. Again, the events of our homely daily life—this time the family life—are depicted against the vast dimensions of time and place. It was written on the eve of our entrance into the war and under strong emotion, and I think it mostly comes alive under conditions of crisis. It has been often charged with being a bookish fantasia about history, full of rather bloodless schoolmasterish jokes. But to have seen it in Germany soon after the war, in the shattered churches and beerhalls that were serving as theatres, with audiences whose price of admission meant the loss of a meal and for whom it was of absorbing interest that there was a "recipe for grass soup that did not cause the diarrhea," was an experience that was not so cool. I am very proud that this year [1957] it has received a first and overwhelming reception in Warsaw. The play is deeply indebted to James Joyce's *Finnegans Wake*. I should be very happy if, in the future, some author should feel similarly indebted to any work of mine. Literature has always more resembled a torch race than a furious dispute among heirs.

The theatre has lagged behind the other arts in finding the "new ways" to express how men and women think and feel in our time. I am not one of the dramatists we are looking for. I wish I were. I hope I have played a part in preparing the way for them. I am not an innovator but a rediscoverer of forgotten goods and I hope a remover of obtrusive bric-a-brac. And as I view the work of my contemporaries I seem to feel that I am exceptional in one thing—I give (don't I?) the impression of having enormously enjoyed it.

WILLIAM INGE

The Taste of Success

THE EXPERIENCE of my first production on Broadway was frantic and bewildering. The play was *Come Back, Little Sheba*, and it was a modest success. I had always hoped for an overwhelming success, but I felt myself very satisfied at the time that *Sheba* had come off as well as it did. Anticipating success (of any degree), I had always expected to feel hilarious, but I didn't. Other people kept coming to me saying, "Aren't you thrilled?" Even my oldest friends, who had known me during the years when I gave myself no peace for lack of success, were baffled by me. There was absolutely no one to understand how I felt, for I didn't feel anything at all. I was in a funk. Where was the joy I had always imagined? Where were the gloating satisfactions I had always anticipated? I looked everywhere to find them. None were there.

A few weeks after *Sheba* opened, a newspaper woman from the Midwest came dancing into my apartment to interview me, bringing with her a party spirit that could not counter with my persisting solemnity. "Where's the celebration?" she wanted to know, looking about the room as though for confetti. "Where's the champagne?" I knew I was not meeting success in the expected way but I was too tired to fake it. I endured her disappointment in me. I could tell by her twitching features that she was wondering what in the world she would tell her readers. Obviously, she couldn't tell them the truth, that the man who had written a (modestly) successful play was one of the saddest-looking creatures she had ever seen. But she didn't let the facts bother her. She returned home and wrote of the play's success and my reaction to it in a fitting way that wouldn't let her readers down. At the time I was too depressed to care.

Other people, friends and acquaintances, couldn't imagine why I had started being psychoanalyzed at this time. "But you're a success now," they would assure me. "What do you want to get analyzed for?" As though successful people automatically became happy, and psychoanalysis were only a remedy for professional failure. But if the personal rewards of my success were a disillusionment to others, they also were to me. My plays since *Sheba* have been more successful, but none of them has brought me the kind of joy, the hilarity, I had craved as a boy, as a young man, living in Kansas and Missouri back in the thirties and forties. Strange and ironic. Once we find the fruits of success, the taste is nothing like what we had anticipated.

Maybe the sleight of hand is performed during the brief interval of rehearsals, out-of-town tryouts, and opening night. A period of six or more weeks that pack a lifetime of growing up. During that period, the playwright comes to realize, maybe with considerable shock, that the play contains something very vital to him, something of the very essence of his own life. If it is rejected, he can only feel that he is rejected, too. Some part of him has been turned down, cast aside, even laughed at or scorned. If it is accepted, all that becomes him to feel is a deep gratefulness, like a man barely escaping a fatal accident, that he has survived.

All my plays have survived on Broadway. All have met with success in varying degrees. And I feel a fitting gratefulness, because they all represent something of me, some view of life that is peculiarly mine that no one else could offer in quite the same style and form. Success, it seems to me, would be somewhat meaningless if the play were not a personal contribution. The author who creates only for audience consumption is only engaged in a financial enterprise. There must always be room for both kinds of theatre, but it is regrettable that they must always compete together in our commercial theatre. For commercial theatre only builds on what has already been created, contributing only theatre back into the theatre. Creative theatre brings something of life itself, which gives the theatre something new to grow on. But when new life comes to us, we don't always recognize it. New life doesn't always survive on Broadway. It's considered risky.

People still come to me sometimes to tell me how much they admired *Come Back, Little Sheba,* referring to the play as though it had been "a smash hit" (a term which we are too eager to apply to shows). Actually, *Sheba* made out well with about half of the reviewers, its total run being something less than six months. Some of the reviews showed an almost violent repugnance to the play. We did good business for only a few weeks and then houses began to dwindle to the size of tea parties. At one time, the actors all took salary cuts, and I took a cut in my royalties. The show was cheap to run, and so, with a struggle, we survived. We always held a small audience of people who were most devoted to the play and came to see it many times. It is remembered now as "a smash hit" or "a hit," probably because the far greater success of the movie shed more glorious reflections on the play.

Now, I don't see how it could have been otherwise with *Sheba*. It is probably a bad omen if any author's first play is "a smash hit." It takes the slow-moving theatre audience one or two plays by a new author, who brings them something new from life outside the theatre, before they can feel sufficiently comfortable with him to consider fairly what he has to say. A good author insists on being accepted on his own terms, and audiences must bicker awhile before they're willing to give in. One learns not to be resentful about this condition but to credit it to human nature.

I have a tendency, after a play of mine is produced, to look back on it disparagingly, seeing only its faults (before production, I see only its virtues). But after the hiatus of opening night, after enough time passes for me to regard each play seriously, as something finally distinct from myself, I have felt that each one gave me some feeling of personal success, that each one contributed something to the theatre out of my life's experience.

I have never sought to write plays that primarily tell a

story; nor have I sought deliberately to create new forms. I have been most concerned with dramatizing something of the dynamism I myself find in human motivations and behavior. I regard a play as a composition rather than a story, as a distillation of life rather than a narration of it. It is only in this way that I feel myself a real contemporary. *Sheba* is the closest thing to a story play that I have written, and it is the only play of mine that could be said to have two central characters. But even this play was a fabric of life, in which the two characters (Doc and Lola) were species of the environment. After *Sheba,* I sought deliberately to fill a larger canvas, to write plays of an over-all texture that made fuller use of the stage as a medium. I strive to keep the stage bubbling with a restless kind of action that seeks first one outlet and then another before finally resolving itself. I like to keep several stories going at once, and to keep as much of the playing area on stage as alive as possible. I use one piece of action to comment on another, not to distract from it. I don't suppose that in any of my later plays I found the single dramatic intensity of action that I found in the drunk scene in *Sheba,* in which Doc threatens Lola's life. I have deliberately sought breadth instead of depth in my plays since *Sheba,* and have sought a more forthright humor than *Sheba* could afford.

In an article I once wrote on *Picnic,* I compared a play to a journey, in which every moment should be as interesting as the destination. I despair of a play that requires its audience to sit through two hours of plot construction, having no reference outside the immediate setting, just to be rewarded by a big emotional pay-off in the last act. This, I regard as a kind of false stimulation. I think every line and every situation in a play should "pay off," too, and have its extensions of meaning beyond the immediate setting, into life. I strive to bring meaning to every moment, every action.

I doubt if my plays "pay off" for an audience unless they are watched rather closely. Writing for a big audience, I deal with surfaces in my plays, and let whatever depths there are in my material emerge unexpectedly so that they bring something of the suddenness and shock which accompany the discovery of truths in actuality. I suppose none of my plays means anything much unless seen as a composite, for I seek dramatic values in a relative way. That is, one character in a play of mine might seem quite pointless unless seen in comparison with another character. For instance, in *Bus Stop,* the cowboy's eagerness, awkwardness, and naïveté in seeking love were interesting only when seen by comparison, in the same setting, with the amorality of Cherie, the depravity of the professor, the casual earthiness of Grace and Carl, the innocence of the schoolgirl Elma, and the defeat of his buddy Virgil. In themselves, the characters may have been entertaining, but not very meaningful.

Bus Stop, I suppose, has less real story than any play that ever survived on Broadway. I meant it only as a composite picture of varying kinds of love, ranging from the innocent to the depraved. With the play's success, I felt quite proud of the fact that I had held the audience's interest long after what would normally be considered the final "pay-off" (when the cowboy and his girl are reunited and go off together). I guess maybe I was trying to prove that a play's merits can exist, not in the dramatization of one soul-satisfying event, but in the over-all pattern and texture of the play. I insisted that the audience be just as interested in what happened to all the characters as they were in Bo and Cherie.

I was sure enough of my craft by the time I started writing *The Dark at the Top of the Stairs* to be able to take my craftsmanship more easily for granted. This play was developed out of the first play I ever wrote, called *Farther Off From Heaven.* Margo Jones produced it in her Dallas theatre in June, 1947, and I didn't know what to do with it at the time but felt it contained too much good material to keep on the shelf. I had been working on the play off and on for over six years, then in the winter of 1957, settled down on it for serious. It is formed from pretty nostalgic memories of childhood, without being very autobiographical. I suppose it represents my belated attempt to come to terms with the past, to rearrange its parts and make them balance, to bring a mature understanding to everyday phenomena that mystified me as a boy. Again, the story is very slight. I deliberately divert the audience from the main story in order to bring them back to it at the end of the play with a fresher viewpoint. In the play, I try to explore some of man's hidden fear in facing life and to show something of the hidden fears that motivate us all. There is a suicide in the play, of a young, homeless, part Jewish boy who has no sure connection with anyone in the world. Some people felt upon reading the play, and others upon first seeing it, that the announcement of the suicide came as too much of a shock; but every suicide I ever heard of came to me in the same way, with no preparation. I have never heard of a suicide that I expected. We always find the reasons for such events after they happen, in re-exploring the character to find motivations we had previously overlooked. It was this kind of dynamism I wanted most to achieve. And I felt also that maybe I was drawing a little on Christian theology to show something of the uniting effect human suffering can bring into our lives.

The success of these four plays, I must share in each case with my director. This is not just a pleasant compliment. I have come to learn how important good direction is to a play, and to realize that good directors are as scarce as good playwrights. I was most fortunate in finding Daniel Mann, unknown at the time, to do *Sheba.* He sensed all the play's implied values and projected them superbly. Joshua Logan, with *Picnic,* was my second director. We had our ups and downs with that play, which I attribute mainly to my second-play nervousness and indecision. An unstable author, who isn't sure what he wants, is a great liability to a director; so if *Picnic* did not come off entirely to please me (as rumor had it), it was my own fault. Josh only sensed my indecision and tried to compensate for it. Still, I feel *Picnic* was a good show. Josh gave it lovely picturesqueness (he is perhaps the most visual of all directors) and feeling of size. I worked on the play with him for a year and a half, during which time he gave of himself very spontaneously. I can never cease being grateful for all that I learned from him.

Harold Clurman is the only real intellectual I know in the theatre. He seems to me a man who has channeled very powerful emotions into a vitally rational life. I was a little dubious about taking *Bus Stop* to him. I didn't see how he, the most metropolitan man I know, could bring understanding to the play's rural types. But he understood them perfectly, I felt, as though by contrast with himself. And he gave me a beautifully felt production.

Working with Elia Kazan sometimes borders on the supernatural; he intuitively senses so quickly all the dim feelings about a play that lie in an author's subconscious. During production, he is the gentlest, humblest man I've ever known. He talks with actors like a ministering angel, infusing them with courage and insight. His range of understanding is from the most delicately sensitive to the most cataclysmically violent. He is a great creative talent.

I also feel very indebted to the superb actors who have taken part in my plays. I would like to list them here, but I truly would not know where to stop in compiling the list. Anyway, I am deeply grateful for the many talented people who have given of their own freshness and vitality to the parts I have written. If there have been poor performances in my plays, I don't recall them now.

"Success is counted sweetest by those who ne'er succeed," according to Emily Dickinson, and I realize what she meant when I compare the success I once anticipated with the success I found. They are not the same things, at all. But the four plays . . . represent almost a decade in my life, a decade that was very intensely lived. Publishing the plays now is like tying those years together to file away, years in which I managed to find some expression for my life and experience, and to find response. Maybe this is all that success means.

ARTHUR MILLER

The Shadows of the Gods

I SEE by the papers that I am going to talk today on the subject of the literary influences on my work. It is probably a good subject, but it isn't what Harold Clurman and I discussed when he asked if I would speak here. What he had in mind was something else. I am supposed to widen your horizons by telling something about the frame of reference I used when I started to write, and that included books I read, or music I heard, or what not.

I doubt whether anybody can widen horizons by making a speech. It is possible, perhaps, by writing a play. Still, I may be able to suggest an approach to our theatre which —even if it is not valid for everyone—will not be quite the same as that of the various critics; and if nothing else is accomplished here maybe it will at least appear that there is another way of looking at drama.

Tolstoy wrote a book called *What Is Art?* The substance of it is that almost all the novels, plays, operas, and paintings were not art but vanity, and that the rhythm with which a Russian peasant swung a scythe was more artful than all the dance on Moscow stages, and the paintings of peasants on the sides of their wagons more genuine than all the paintings in the museums. The thing that disheartened him most, I believe, was that inevitably artistic creation became a profession, and the artist who may have originated as a natural quickly became self-conscious and

Copyright © 1958 by *Harper's Magazine*. Reprinted by permission. The essay is to be found in *Harper's Magazine,* CCXVII (August, 1958), 35–43. The speech was delivered before a meeting of the New Dramatists Committee in the spring of 1958.

exploited his own gifts for money, prestige, or just for want of an honest profession.

Yet, Tolstoy went on writing. The truth, I suppose, is that soon or late we are doomed to know what we are doing, and we may as well accept it as a fact when it comes. But the self-knowledge of professionalism develops only as a result of having repeated the same themes in different plays. And for a whole theatre the time for self-appraisal comes in the same way. We are, I believe, at the end of a period. Certain things have been repeated sufficiently for one to speak of limitations which have to be recognized if our theatre is not to become absurd, repetitious, and decayed.

Now one can no sooner speak of limitations than the question of standards arises. What seems like a limitation to one man may be an area as wide as the world to another. My standard, my viewpoint, whether it appears arbitrary, or true and inevitable, did not spring out of my head un-shaped by any outside force. I began writing plays in the midst of what Allan Seager, an English teacher friend of mine at Michigan, calls one of the two genuinely national catastrophes in American history—the Great Depression of the thirties. The other was the Civil War. It is almost bad manners to talk about depression these days, but through no fault or effort of mine it was the ground upon which I learned to stand.

There are a thousand things to say about that time but maybe one will be evocative enough. Until 1929 I thought things were pretty solid. Specifically, I thought—like most Americans—that somebody was in charge. I didn't know exactly who it was, but it was probably a business man, and he was a realist, a no-nonsense fellow, practical, honest, responsible. In 1929 he jumped out of the window. It was bewildering. His banks closed and refused to open again, and I had twelve dollars in one of them. More precisely, I happened to have withdrawn my twelve dollars to buy a racing bike a friend of mine was bored with, and the next day the Bank of the United States closed. I rode by and saw the crowds of people standing at the brass gates. Their money was inside. And they couldn't get it. And they would never get it. As for me, I felt I had the thing licked.

But about a week later I went into the house to get a glass of milk and when I came out my bike was gone. Stolen. It must have taught me a lesson. Nobody could escape that disaster.

I did not read many books in those days. The depression was my book. Years later I could put together what in those days were only feelings, sensations, impressions. There was the sense that everything had dried up. Some plague of invisible grasshoppers was eating money before you could get your hands on it. You had to be a Ph.D. to get a job in Macy's. Lawyers were selling ties. Everybody was trying to sell something to everybody else. A past president of the Stock Exchange was sent to jail for misappropriating trust funds. They were looking for runaway financiers all over Europe and South America. Practically everything that had been said and done up to 1929 turned out to be a fake. It turns out that there had never been anybody in charge.

What the time gave me, I think now, was a sense of an invisible world. A reality had been secretly accumulating its climax according to its hidden laws to explode illusion at the proper time. In that sense 1929 was our Greek year. The gods had spoken, the gods whose wisdom had been set aside or distorted by a civilization that was to go onward and upward on speculation, gambling, graft, and the dog eating the dog. Before the crash I thought "Society" meant the rich people in the Social Register. After the crash it meant the constant visits of strange men who knocked on our door pleading for a chance to wash the windows, and some of them fainted on the back porch from hunger. In Brooklyn, New York. In the light of weekday afternoons.

I read books after I was seventeen, but already, for good or ill, I was not patient with every kind of literature. I did not believe, even then, that you could tell about a man without telling about the world he was living in, what he did for a living, what he was like not only at home or in bed but on the job. I remember now reading novels and wondering, What do these people do for a living? When do they work? I remember asking the same questions about the few plays I saw. The hidden laws of fate lurked not only in the characters of people, but equally if not more imperiously in the world beyond the family parlor. Out there were the big gods, the ones whose disfavor could turn a proud and prosperous and dignified man into a frightened shell of a man whatever he thought of himself, and whatever he decided or didn't decide to do.

So that by force of circumstance I came early and unawares to be fascinated by sheer process itself. How things connected. How the native personality of a man was changed by his world, and the harder question, how he could in turn change his world. It was not academic. It was not even a literary or a dramatic question at first. It was the practical problem of what to believe in order to proceed with life. For instance, should one admire success—for there were successful people even then. Or should one always see through it as an illusion which only existed to be blown up, and its owner destroyed and humiliated. Was success immoral?—when everybody else in the neighborhood not only had no Buick but no breakfast? What to believe?

An adolescent must feel he is on the side of justice. That is how human indignation is constantly renewed. But how hard it was to feel justly, let alone to think justly. There were people in the neighborhood saying that it had all happened because the workers had not gotten paid enough to buy what they had produced, and that the solution was to have Socialism, which would not steal their wages any more the way the bosses did and brought on this depression. It was a wonderful thought with which I nearly drove my grandfather crazy. The trouble with it was that he and my father and most of the men I loved would have to be destroyed.

Enough of that. I am getting at only one thought. You can't understand anything unless you understand its relations to its context. It was necessary to feel beyond the edges of things. That much, for good or ill, the Great Depression taught me. It made me impatient with anything, including art, which pretends that it can exist for its own sake and still be of any prophetic importance. A thing becomes beautiful to me as it becomes internally and externally organic. It becomes beautiful because it promises

to remove some of my helplessness before the chaos of
experience. I think one of the reasons I became a playwright was that in dramatic form everything must be
openly organic, deeply organized, articulated from a living
center. I used long ago to keep a book in which I would
talk to myself. One of the aphorisms I wrote was, "The
structure of a play is always the story of how the birds
came home to roost." The hidden will be unveiled; the
inner laws of reality will announce themselves; I was defin-
ing my impression of 1929 as well as dramatic structure.

When I was still in high school and ignorant, a book
came into my hands, God knows how, *The Brothers Ka-
ramazov*. It must have been too rainy that day to play
ball. I began reading it thinking it was a detective story.
I had always blessed Dostoevski for writing in a way that
any fool could understand. The book, of course, has no
connection with the depression. Yet it became closer, more
intimate to me, despite the Russian names, than the papers
I read every day. I never thought to ask why, then. I think
now it was because of the father and son conflict, but
something more. It is always probing beyond its particular
scenes and characters for the hidden laws, for the place
where the gods ruminate and decide, for the rock upon
which one may stand without illusion, a free man. Yet the
characters appear liberated from any systematic causation.
The same yearning I felt all day for some connection
with a hidden logic was the yearning in this book. It gave
me no answers but it showed that I was not the only one
who was full of this kind of questioning, for I did not
believe—and could not after 1929—in the reality I saw
with my eyes. There was an invisible world of cause and
effect, mysterious, full of surprises, implacable in its course.
The book said to me: "There is a hidden order in the
world. There is only one reason to live. It is to discover
its nature. The good are those who do this. The evil say
that there is nothing beyond the face of the world, the
surface of reality. Man will only find peace when he learns
to live humanly, in conformity to those laws which decree
his human nature."

Only slightly less ignorant, I read Ibsen in college. Later I heard that I had been reading problem plays. I didn't know what that meant. I was told they were about social problems like the inequality of women. The women I knew about had not been even slightly unequal; I saw no such problem in *A Doll's House*. I connected with Ibsen not because he wrote about problems, but because he was illuminating process. Nothing in his plays exists for itself, not a smart line, not a gesture that can be isolated. It was breath-taking.

From his work—read again and again with new wonders cropping up each time—as well as through Dostoevski's, I came to an idea of what a writer was supposed to be. These two issued the license, so to speak, the only legitimate one I could conceive, for presuming to write at all. One had the right to write because other people needed news of the inner world, and if they went too long without such news they would go mad with the chaos of their lives. With the greatest of presumption I conceived that the great writer was the destroyer of chaos, a man privy to the councils of the hidden gods who administer the hidden laws that bind us all and destroy us if we do not know them. And chaos, for one thing, was life lived oblivious of history.

As time went on, a lot of time, it became clear to me that I was not only reporting to others but to myself first and foremost. I wrote not only to find a way into the world but to hold it away from me so that sheer, senseless events would not devour me.

I read the Greeks and the German Expressionists at the same time and quite by accident. I was struck by the similarity of their dramatic means in one respect—they are designed to present the hidden forces, not the characteristics of the human beings playing out those forces on the stage. I was told that the plays of Aeschylus must be read primarily on a religious level, that they are only lay dramas to us now because we no longer believe. I could not understand this because one did not have to be religious to see in our own disaster the black outlines of a fate that was not human, nor of the heavens either, but something in between. Like the howling of a mob, for instance, which is not a human sound but is nevertheless composed of human voices combining until a metaphysical force of sound is created.

I read O'Neill in those days as I read everything else— looking to see how meaning was achieved. He said something in a press conference which in the context of those years seemed to be a challenge to the social preoccupations of the thirties. He said, "I am not interested in the relations of man to man, but of man to God." I thought that very reactionary. Until, after repeated and repeated forays into one play of my own after another, I understood that he meant what I meant, not ideologically but dramatically speaking. I too had a religion, however unwilling I was to be so backward. A religion with no gods but with godlike powers. The powers of economic crisis and political imperatives which had twisted, torn, eroded, and marked everything and everyone I laid eyes on.

I read for a year in economics, discovered my professors dispensing their prejudices which were no better founded than my own; worse yet, an economics that could measure the giant's footsteps but could not look into his eyes.

I read for a year in history, and lost my last illusion on a certain afternoon at two-thirty. In a lecture class a student at question time rose to ask the professor if he thought Hitler would invade Austria. For fifteen minutes the professor, by no means a closet historian but a man of liberal and human interests, proved why it was impossible for Hitler to invade Austria. It seems there were treaties forbidding this which went back to the Congress of Vienna, side agreements older than that, codicils, memoranda, guarantees—and to make a long story short, when we got out at three o'clock there was an extra being hawked. Hitler had invaded Austria. I gave up history. I knew damned well Hitler was going to invade Austria.

In that sense it was a good time to be growing up because nobody else knew anything either. All the rules were nothing but continuations of older rules. The old plays create new plays, and the old histories create new histories. The best you could say of the academic disciplines was that they were breathlessly running after the world. It is when life creates a new play that the theatre moves its limbs and wakens from its mesmerized fixation on ordinary reality; when the present is caught and made historic.

I began by speaking of standards. I have labored the point long enough to state it openly. My standard is, to be sure, derived from my life in the thirties, but I believe that it is as old as the drama itself and was merely articulated to me in the accent of the thirties. I ask of a play, first, the dramatic question, the carpenter-builder's question—What is its ultimate force? How can that force be released? Second, the human question—What is its ultimate relevancy to the survival of the race?

Before proceeding with these two queries I want to jump ahead to say that my object remains to throw some light on our dramatic situation today, the challenge, so to speak, which I think lies before us. I will pause for a moment or two in order to say a few things about a writer who has been, along with Ibsen, an enormous influence upon our theatre whether we know it or not.

It is hard to imagine any playwright reading Chekhov without envying one quality of his plays. It is his balance. In this, I think he is closer to Shakespeare than any dramatist I know. There is less distortion by the exigencies of the telescoping of time in the theatre, there is less stacking of the cards, there is less fear of the ridiculous, there is less fear of the heroic. His touch is tender, his eye is warm, so warm that the Chekhovian legend in our theatre has become that of an almost sentimental man and writer whose plays are elegies, postscripts to a dying age. In passing, it must be said that he was not the only Russian writer who seemed to be dealing with all his characters as though he were related to them. It is a quality not of Chekhov alone but of much Russian literature, and I mention it both to relate him to this mood and to separate him from it.

Chekhov is important to us because he has been used as a club against two opposing views of drama. Sometimes he seems—as he evidently does to Walter Kerr—to have encouraged dramatists to an overly-emphasized introspection if not self-pity. To this kind of viewpoint, he is the playwright of inaction, of perverse self-analysis, of the

dark blue mood. In the thirties he was condemned by
many on the Left as lacking in militancy, and he was
confused with the people he was writing about.

His plays, I think, will endure, but in one sense he is as
useless as a model as the frock coat and the horse and
carriage. Our civilization is immeasurably more strident
than his and to try to recreate his mood would be to distort
our own. But more important, I think, is that—whatever
the miseries of his characters—their careers are played out
against a tradition of which they are quite conscious, a
tradition whose destruction is regarded by them as the
setting of their woes. Whether or not it was ever objectively
true is beside the point, of course; the point is that they can
look back to a time when the coachman was young and
happy to be a coachman, when there was a large, firmly
entrenched family evenly maturing over the slow-passing
years, when, in a word, there was an order dominated by
human relations. Now—to put it much more briefly than its
complexity warrants—the Cherry Orchard is cut down by
a real-estate man, who, nice fellow that he may be, simply
has to clear land for a development.

The closest we have ever gotten to this kind of relation
to a tradition is in Tennessee Williams, when a disorgan-
ized refugee from a plantation arrives in our civilization
some eighty years after the plantation itself has been destroyed. We cannot reproduce Chekhov if only because we
are long past the time when we believe in the primacy of
human relations over economic necessity. We have given
up what was still in his time a live struggle. We believe—
or at least take it completely for granted—that wherever
there is a conflict between human relations and necessity,
the outcome is not only inevitable but even progressive
when necessity wins, as it evidently must.

The main point I would make here in relation to our
theatre, however, is that while Chekhov's psychological
insight is given full play, and while his greatest interest is
overwhelmingly in the spiritual life of his characters, his
farthest vision does not end with their individual psychology. Here is a speech to remind you—and it is only one
of a great many which do not at all fit with the conventional characterization of these allegedly wispy plays—

concerned with nothing more than realistic character drawing and introspection. In *Three Sisters* Vershinin speaks:

> What else am I to say to you at parting? What am I to theorize about? (*Laughs*) Life is hard. It seems to many of us blank and hopeless; but yet we must admit that it goes on getting clearer and easier, and it looks as though the time were not far off when it will be full of happiness. (*Looks at his watch.*) It's time for me to go! In the old days men were absorbed in wars, filling all their existence with marches, raids, victories, but now all that is a thing of the past, leaving behind it a great void which there is so far nothing to fill; humanity is searching for it passionately, and of course will find it. Ah, if only it could be quickly. If, don't you know, industry were united with culture and culture with industry. . . . (*Looks at his watch.*) But, I say, it's time for me to go. . . .

In other words, these plays are not mere exercises in psychology. They are woven around a very critical point of view, a point of view not only toward the characters, but toward the social context in which they live, a point of view which—far from being some arbitrary angle, as we have come to call such things—is their informing principle. I haven't the time here to investigate the plays one by one and it is not the business of the moment. All I have said comes down to this: that with all our technical dexterity, with all our lighting effects, sets, and a theatre more solvent than any I know about, yes, with all our freedom to say what we will—our theatre is narrowing its vision year by year, it is repeating well what it has done well before.

I can hear already my critics complaining that I am asking for a return to what they call problem plays. That criticism is important only because it tells something important about the critic. It means that he can only conceive of man as a private entity, and his social relations as something thrown at him, something "affecting" him only when he is conscious of society. I hope I have made one thing clear to this point—and it is that society is inside of man and man is inside society, and you cannot even create a truthfully drawn psychological entity on the stage until you understand his social relations and their power to make him what he is and to prevent him from being

what he is not. The fish is in the water and the water is
in the fish.

I believe we have arrived in America at the end of a
period because we are repeating ourselves season after
season, despite the fact that nobody seems to be aware of it.
In almost every success there is a striking similarity of
mood and of mode. There is one play after another in
which a young person, usually male, usually sensitive, is
driven either to self-destructive revolt or impotency by the
insensitivity of his parents, usually the father. A quick
and by no means exhaustive look brings to mind, *Look
Homeward, Angel, Dark at the Top of the Stairs, Cat on
a Hot Tin Roof, A Hatful of Rain*. I wish to emphasize at
once that I am not here as a critic of these plays as plays,
nor do I intend to equate their worth one with the other. I
am rather looking at them as a stranger, a man from Mars,
who would surely have to wonder at so pervasive a phenomenon.

Now I am not saying there is anything "wrong" with
this theme, if only because I have written more than
once on it myself. It lies at the heart of all human development, and its echoes go to *Hamlet,* to *Romeo and Juliet,*
to *Oedipus Rex*. What I am critical of is that our theatre
is dealing almost exclusively with affects. Where the parent
stands the world ends, and where the son stands is where
the world should begin but cannot because he is either made
impotent, or he revolts, or more often runs away. What
is there wrong with this? Does it not happen all the time?
It must, or so many playwrights would not be repeating
the theme, and it would not have the fascination it evidently does for so many audiences.

What is wrong is not the theme but its failure to extend
itself so as to open up ultimate causes. The fact, for one
thing, is not merely the frustration of the children, or even
the bankruptcy of moral authority in the parents, but also
their common awareness in our time of some hidden,
ulterior causation for this. If only because this theme is so
recurrent, the phenomenon has the right to be called a
generalized social one. Therefore, it is proper in this instance to say that the potential vision of these plays is not

fulfilled and their potential aesthetic size and perfection is left unrealized. And perhaps even more important, there is implicit in this cut-down vision a decay of nerve, a withering of power to grasp the whole world on the stage and shake it to its foundations as it is the historic job of high drama to do. The mystery of our condition remains, but we know much more about it than appears on our stage.

I am not asking for anything new, but something as old as the Greek drama. When Chekhov, that almost legendary subjectivist, has Vershinin—and many others in his plays —objectifying the social questions which his play has raised, he is merely placing himself within the great tradition which set its art works fully in view of the question of the survival of the race. It is we who are the innovators, or more precisely, the sports, when we refuse to reflect on our stage a level of objective awareness at least as great as exists commonly in our lives outside.

I am asking for the world to be brought into the stage family, to be sure, but I begin and I end from the viewpoint of the dramatist, the dramatist seeking to intensify the power of his plays and his theatre. There is something dramatically wrong, for instance, when an audience can see a play about the Nazi treatment of a group of Jews hiding in an attic, and come away feeling the kind of— I can only call it gratification—which the audiences felt after seeing *The Diary of Anne Frank*. Seeing this play, I was not only an audience or even a Jew, but a dramatist, and it puzzled me why it was all so basically reassuring to watch what must have been the most harrowing kind of suffering in real life.

As a constructor of plays I had nothing technical of consequence to add. And I found myself putting to this play the question I have put to you—What is its relevancy to the survival of the race? Not the American race, or the Jewish race, or the German race, but the human race. And I believe the beginning of an answer has emerged. It is that with all its truth the play lacks the kind of spread vision, the over-vision beyond its characters and their problems, which could have illuminated not merely the cruelty of Nazism but something even more terrible. We see no

Nazis in this play. Again, as with the plays I have mentioned, it is seen from the viewpoint of the adolescent, a poignant and human viewpoint to be sure, but surely a limited one. The approach of the Nazi is akin to the approach of a childhood Demon.

What was necessary in this play to break the hold of reassurance upon the audience, and to make it match the truth of life, was that we should see the bestiality in our own hearts, so that we should know how we are brothers not only to these victims but to the Nazis, so that the ultimate terror of our lives should be faced—namely our own sadism, our own ability to obey orders from above, our own fear of standing firm on humane principle against the obscene power of the mass organization. Another dimension was waiting to be opened up behind this play, a dimension covered with our own sores, a dimension revealing us to ourselves.

Once this dimension had been unveiled we could not have watched in the subtly perverse comfort of pathos; our terror would no longer be for these others but for ourselves, once that part of ourselves which covertly conspires with destruction was made known. Then, for one thing, even tragedy would have been possible, for the issue would not have been why the Nazis were so cruel, but why human beings—ourselves, us—are so cruel. The pathetic is the refusal or inability to discover and face ultimate relevancy for the race; it is therefore a shield against ultimate dramatic effect.

In this instance the objection will be raised that I am demanding a different kind of play than *Diary* was intended to be. I am. I make this demand, if one can presume so far, even though I believe that the original book was very faithfully followed by the dramatists who adapted it. Who am I to argue with the martyred girl who wrote the original document? Her right to her point of view is irreproachable. I agree that it is irreproachable. I repeat, as a matter of fact, what I said earlier—that the adolescent viewpoint is and should be precious to us. In this instance, first of all, I am treating the play as a separate work, as another play opening in New York. Secondly, I am using it to show that even when the adolescent viewpoint is most perfectly announced and movingly dramatized, it nevertheless has a nature, an inner dynamic which prevents it from seeing what it cannot see and still be itself.

It is necessary, in short, to be able to appreciate a thing for what it is, and to see what it is not and what it might be. Our present failure to distinguish between low and high altitude, between amplitude and relative narrowness, leaves us—as it leaves the critics for the most part—at the mercy of "affects"; which is to say that if a small play of minor proportions achieves its affects well, it is as good as a large play of greater proportions.

One consequence of this inability to distinguish between the sizes of things, so to speak, is to condemn ourselves ultimately to minor art. For it is always more likely that small things of shallow breath will show fewer defects than the large, and if the perfecting of affects, regardless of their larger relevancies or irrelevancies, is to be our criterion, as it threatens now to be, we shall turn our theatre into a kind of brooding conceit, a showplace for our tricks, a proving ground for our expertise, a shallows protected from the oceans.

I repeat that I am not here as a critic of individual plays but of the dramatic viewpoint which I believe imposes by no means unbreakable limitations upon them. They are limitations which tend to force repetitions of mood, mode, style, yes, and even the lighting and settings of one play after another, even as they are written, by writers in their individual isolation. While on the one hand we prize the original work, the new creation, we are surprisingly unconscious of the sameness of so much that passes for new. But the new, the truly new dramatic poem will be, as it has always been, a new organization of the meaning, the generalized significance of the action.

A moment ago I threw together several plays for the purposes of this discussion, one of which I should like now to set apart. In every way but one *Cat on a Hot Tin Roof* differs from *Diary of Anne Frank,* as well as from the others mentioned. Williams has a long reach and a genuinely dramatic imagination. To me, however, his greatest value, his aesthetic valor, so to speak, lies in his very evident determination to unveil and engage the widest range of causation conceivable to him. He is constantly pressing his own limit. He creates shows, as all of us must, but he possesses the restless inconsolability with his solutions which is inevitable in a genuine writer. In my opinion, he is properly discontented with the total image some of his plays have created. And it is better that way, for when the image is complete and self-contained it is usually arbitrary and false.

It is no profound thing to say that a genuine work of art creates not completion, but a sustained image of things in tentative balance. What I say now is not to describe that balance as a false or illusory one, but one whose weighing containers, so to speak, are larger and greater than what has been put into them. I think, in fact, that in *Cat on a Hot Tin Roof*, Williams in one vital respect made an assault upon his own viewpoint in an attempt to break it up and reform it on a wider circumference.

Essentially it is a play seen from the viewpoint of Brick, the son. He is a lonely young man sensitized to injustice. Around him is a world whose human figures partake in various ways of grossness, Philistinism, greed, money-lust, power-lust. And—with his mean-spirited brother as an example—it is a world senselessly reproducing itself through ugly children conceived without the grace of genuine affection, and delivered not so much as children but as inheritors of great wealth and power, the new perpetuators of inequity.

In contrast, Brick conceives of his friendship with his dead friend as an idealistic, even gallant and valorous and somehow morally elevated one, a relationship in which nothing was demanded, but what was given was given unasked, beyond the realm of price, of value, even of materiality. He clings to this image as to a banner of purity to flaunt against the world, and more precisely, against the decree of nature to reproduce himself, to become in turn the father, the master of the earth, the administrator of the tainted and impure world. It is a world in whose relations—especially between the sexes—there is always the element of the transaction, of materiality.

If the play confined itself to the psychiatry of impotence,

it could be admired or dismissed as such. Williams' plays are never really that, but here in addition, unlike his other plays, there is a father. Not only is he the head of the family, but the very image of power, of materiality, of authority. And the problem this father is given is how he can infuse his own personality into the prostrated spirit of his son so that a hand as strong as his own will guide his fortune when he is gone—more particularly, so that his own immortality, his civilization will be carried on.

As the play was produced, without the surface realism of living room, bedroom, walls, conventional light—in an atmosphere, instead, of poetic conflict, in a world that is eternal and not merely this world—it provided more evidence that Williams' preoccupation extends beyond the surface realities of the relationships, and beyond the psychiatric connotations of homosexuality and impotence. In every conceivable fashion there was established a goal beyond sheer behavior. We were made to see, I believe, an ulterior pantheon of forces and a play of symbols as well as of characters.

It is well known that there was difficulty in ending this play, and I am certainly of no mind to try it. I believe I am not alone in saying that the resolution wherein Brick finally regains potency was not understandable on the stage. But my feeling is that even if this were more comprehensibly motivated so that the psychiatric development of the hero were persuasively completed, it in itself could not embrace the other questions raised in the play.

We are persuaded as we watch this play that the world around Brick is in fact an unworthy collection of unworthy motives and greedy actions. Brick refuses to participate in this world, but he cannot destroy it either or reform it and he turns against himself. The question here, it seems to me, the ultimate question is the right of society to renew itself when it is, in fact, unworthy. There is, after all, a highly articulated struggle for material power going on here. There is literally and symbolically a world to win or a world to forsake and damn. A viewpoint is necessary, if one is to raise such a tremendous issue, a viewpoint capable of encompassing it. This is not a study in cynicism where the writer merely exposes the paradoxes of all sides and is content to end with a joke. Nor, again, is it mere psychiatry, aiming to show us how a young man reclaims his sexuality. There is a moral judgment hanging over this play which never quite comes down. A tempting analogy would be that of a Hamlet who takes up his sword and neither fights nor refuses to fight but marries an Ophelia who does not die.

Brick, despite his resignation from the race, has thrown a challenge to it which informs the whole play, a challenge which the father and the play both recognize and ignore. But if it is the central challenge of the play—as the play seems to me to emphasize—then the world must either prove its worthiness to survive, or its unworthiness must lie dramatically proved, to justify Brick's refusal to renew it— or, like a Hamlet who will neither do battle nor put down his sword, it must condemn Brick to inaction and perhaps indifference to its fate.

Because of Williams' marvelous ability, I for one would be willing to listen—and perhaps to him alone—even as he pronounced ultimate doom upon the race—a race exemplified in his play by the meanest of motives. This is a foundation grand enough, deep enough, and worthy of being examined remorselessly and perhaps even shaken and smashed. Again, as with *The Diary of Anne Frank,* had the implicit challenge ripened, we should no longer be held by our curiosity or our pity for someone else, but by that terror which comes when we must in truth justify our most basic assumptions. The father in this play, I think, must be forced to the wall in justification of his world, and Brick must be forced to his wall in justification of his condemning that world to the ultimate biological degree. The question of society's right to insist upon its renewal when it is unworthy is a question of tragic grandeur, and those who have asked this question of the world know full well the lash of its retaliation.

Quite simply, what I am asking is that the play pursue the ultimate development of the very questions it asks. But for such a pursuit, the viewpoint of the adolescent is not enough. The father, with the best will in the world, *is* faced with the problem of a son he loves best refusing to accept him and his spirit. Worse yet, it is to the least worthy son that that spirit must be handed if all else fails. Above the father's and the son's individual viewpoints the third must emerge, the viewpoint, in fact, of the audience, the society, and the race. It is a viewpoint that must weigh, as I have said, the question of its own right to biological survival—and one thing more, the question of the fate of the sensitive and the just in an impure world of power. After all, ultimately someone must take charge; this is the tragic dilemma, but it is beyond the viewpoint of adolescence. Someone must administer inequity or himself destroy that world by refusing to renew it, or by doing battle against its injustice, or by declaring his indifference or his cynicism. The terms upon which Brick's potency returns are left waiting to be defined and the play is thus torn from its climax.

Again, I am not criticizing this play, but attempting to mark the outlines of its viewpoint—which is an extension of our theatre's viewpoint—to its present limits. Nor is this an entirely new and unheralded idea. Be it Tolstoy, Dostoevski, Hemingway, you, or I, we are formed in this world when we are sons and daughters and the first truths we know throw us into conflict with our fathers and mothers. The struggle for mastery—for the freedom of manhood or womanhood as opposed to the servility of childhood—is the struggle not only to overthrow authority but to reconstitute it anew. The viewpoint of the adolescent is precious because it is revolutionary and insists upon justice. But in truth the parent, powerful as he appears, is not the source of injustice but its deputy.

A drama which refuses or is unable to reach beyond this façade is denying itself its inherited chance for greatness. The best of our theatre is standing tiptoe, striving to see over the shoulders of father and mother. The worst is exploiting and wallowing in the self-pity of adolescence and obsessive keyhole sexuality. The way out, as the poet has said, is always *through*. We will not find it by huddling closer to the center of the charmed circle, by developing more and more naturalism in our dialogue and our acting, that "slice-of-life" reportage which is to life what an overheard rumor is to truth; nor by setting up an artificial poetic style, nor by once again shocking the householders with yet other unveilings of domestic relations and their hypocrisies. Nor will we break out by writing problem plays. There is an organic aesthetic, a tracking of impulse and causation from the individual to the world and back again which must be reconstituted. We are exhausting the realm of affects, which is the world of adolescence taken pure.

The shadow of a cornstalk on the ground is lovely, but it is no denial of its loveliness to see as one looks on it that it is telling the time of day, the position of the earth and the sun, the size of our planet and its shape, and perhaps even the length of its life and ours among the stars. A viewpoint bounded by affects cannot engage the wider balance of our fates where the great climaxes are found.

In my opinion, if our stage does not come to pierce through affects to an evaluation of the world, it will contract to a lesser psychiatry and an inexpert one at that. We shall be confined to writing on *Oedipus* without the pestilence, an Oedipus whose catastrophe is private and unrelated to the survival of his people, an Oedipus who cannot tear out his eyes because there will be no standard by which he can judge himself; an Oedipus, in a word, who on learning of his incestuous marriage, instead of tearing out his eyes, will merely wipe away his tears thus to declare his loneliness. Again, where a drama will not engage its relevancy for the race, it will halt at pathos, that tempting shield against ultimate dramatic effect, that counterfeit of meaning.

Symbolically, as though sensing that we are confined, we have removed the doors and walls and ceilings from our sets. But the knowing eye still sees them there. They may truly disappear and the stage will open to that symbolic stature, that realm where the father is after all not the final authority, that area where he is the son too, that area where religions are made and the giants live, only when we see beyond parents, who are, after all, but the shadows of the gods.

A great drama is a great jurisprudence. Balance is all. It will evade us until we can once again see man as whole, until sensitivity and power, justice and necessity are utterly face to face, until authority's justifications and rebellion's too are tracked even to those heights where the breath fails, where—because the largest point of view as well as the smaller has spoken—truly the rest is silence.

ARCHIBALD MacLEISH

About a Trespass on a Monument

IF THE invitation to write this piece means that the drama editor of *The New York Times* regards my play [*J. B.*] as crying out, like Job's boils, for justification, I can only agree. A man may be forgiven for dramatizing an incident from the Bible and even for modernizing it in the process. But what I have done is not so easy to excuse. I have constructed a modern play inside the ancient majesty of the Book of Job much as the Bedouins, thirty years ago, used to build within the towering ruins of Palmyra their shacks of gasoline tins roofed with fallen stones.

The Bedouins had the justification of necessity and I can think of nothing better for myself. When you are dealing with questions too large for you, which, nevertheless, will not leave you alone, you are obliged to house them somewhere—and an old wall helps. Which is perhaps why so many modern plays have proved, on critical examination, to be reconstructions of the myths of Greece. That appeal to precedent, however, is of little use to me, for my *J. B.* is not a reconstruction of the Book of Job—not, at least, a reconstruction of the kind presently familiar in which the discovery of the model is part of the adventure. My play is put in motion by two broken-down actors who believe, themselves, that the play is the Book of Job and that one of them is acting God and the other, Satan. When J. B. and his family appear, however, it is not out of the Bible that they come.

But justification is still necessary and necessity is still the

Appeared first in the drama section of *The New York Times* of December 7, 1958, and is reprinted here with the permission of Archibald MacLeish.

only justification I can plead. I badly needed an ancient structure on which to build the contemporary play that has haunted me for five years past, and the structure of the poem of Job is the only one I know of which our modern history will fit. Job's search, like ours, was for the meaning of his afflictions—the loss of his children, the loss of everything he possessed, the loss of his wife's kindness, who turned upon him in his agony with those ineradicable words, surely the most dreadful ever spoken by wife to husband: "Curse God and die!" There was no reason for all this: no reason the mind, at least, could grasp. Job was, by witness of God himself and twice repeated, "a perfect and an upright man" and his destruction was, by the same unquestionable authority, "without cause." As for ourselves, there can be very few of us who are perfect, but the enormous, nameless disasters that have befallen whole cities, entire peoples, in two great wars and many small ones, have destroyed the innocent together with the guilty —and with no "cause" our minds can grasp.

We attribute these sufferings, except when it is we ourselves who have inflicted them, to the malevolence of our enemies, but even so we are appalled by all this anguish. Hiroshima, in its terrible retrospect, appalls us. And we attempt—millions of us, the psychiatrists say—to justify the inexplicable misery of the world by taking the guilt upon ourselves, as Job attempted to take it: "Show me my guilt, O God." We even listen, as Job did, to the Comforters—though our Comforters are not like his. Where Job's Comforters undertook to persuade him, against the evidence of his own inner conviction, that he *was* guilty, ours attempt to persuade us that we are not—that we cannot be—that, for psychological reasons, or because everything is determined in advance by economic necessity anyway, or because we were damned before we started, guilt is impossible. Our Comforters are, if anything, less comfortable than Job's, for they drive us from the last refuge in which our minds can hide from the enormous silence. If we cannot even be guilty, then there are no reasons.

There are those, I know—because I have heard them— who will object that Job's story bears no true relationship to our own because God has changed in the interval. The

God of Job is God the Creator of the Universe, and science, they say, now knows that there is no such Creator—that the events of time progress by an automatism of their own —that the watch winds itself and ticks by its own juggling. The modern God of the scientific age, that is to say, does not control events: not, at least, events in the world of here and now.

I have no wish, and certainly no competence, to argue the questions of faith that underlie that attitude. But two things may be said from the merely human position. The first relates to the statement that science knows now there is no Creator. Does it? Einstein has told us that he had sometimes the sense that he was following, in his plumbings and probings of the universe, the track of an Intelligence far beyond the reaches of his own. The second thing to be said is this: that there has been nothing in human history that has brought mankind closer to the immanence of an infinite creativity than the revelation that the minutest particles of inert matter contain an almost immeasurable power. To me, a man committed to no creed, and more uncertain than I should be of certain ultimate beliefs, the God of Job seems closer to this generation than he has to any other in centuries.

My hero, called J. B. after the current fashion in business address, bears little relation, perhaps, to that ancient owner of camels and oxen and sheep. He is not a particularly devout man. But he is, at the beginning of the play, prosperous, powerful, possessed of a lovely wife, fine children—everything the heart of man can desire—and he is aware, as he could hardly help being, that God has made "an hedge about him and about his house and about all that he hath on every side." Not that the name of God is often in his mouth. He is one of those vastly successful American business men—not as numerous now as they were before the Great Depression—who, having everything, believe as a matter of course that they have a right to have everything. They do not believe this out of vulgarity. They are not Babbitts: on the contrary, they are most often men of exuberance, of high animal spirits, of force and warmth. They believe it because they possess in large measure that characteristically American courage that has so often amused Asian and European visitors, the courage to believe in themselves. Which means to believe in their lives. Which means, if their tongues can shape the words, to believe in God's goodness to them. They are not hypocritical. They do not think that they deserve more at God's hands than others. They merely think that they have more—and that they have a right to have it.

Such a man is no better prepared than Job was for the sudden and inexplicable loss of everything. And such a man must ask, as our time does ask, Job's repeated question. Job wants *justice* of the universe. He needs to know the reason for his wretchedness. And it is in those repeated cries of his that we hear most clearly our own voices. For our age is an age haunted and driven by the need to know. Not only is our science full of it but our arts also. And it is here, or so it seems to me, that our story and the story of Job come closest to each other. Job is not *answered* in the Bible by the voice out of the whirling wind. He is *silenced* by it—silenced by some thirty or forty of the greatest lines in all literature—silenced by the might and majesty and magnificence of the creation. He is brought, not to *know*, but to *see*. As we also have been brought.

And what follows that *seeing* which cannot *know?* What follows is a chapter of the Book of Job the theologians have tried again and again to explain away. Job is given all he had before twice over—all but his children who are the same in number but more beautiful. And that is not all. Not only is Job *given* his life again: Job *accepts* his life again. The man who was once highest and happiest and has now been brought lowest and made most miserable; the man who has suffered every loss, every agony, and for no reason, moral or intelligible, the mind can grasp; the man who has cried out to God for death, begged over and over to die, regretted the womb that bore him, yearned never to have been, never to have breathed the air or seen the light—*this* man accepts his life again, accepts to live his life again, take back his wife again, beget new children mortal as those others, risk himself upon the very hazards on which, before, his hopes were wrecked. And

why? Because his sufferings have been justified? They have
not been justified. God has merely lifted into the blazing
fire of the imagination his own power and Job's impotence;
his own immeasurable knowledge and Job's poor, trembling, ridiculous ignorance. Job accepts to live his life
again in spite of all he knows of life, in spite of all he
knows now of himself, because he is a man.

Our own demand for justice and for reasons comes to
the same unanswering answer. A few days before he died,
the greatest of modern poets, and the most modern of great
poets, William Butler Yeats, wrote to a friend that he had
found what, all his life, he had been looking for. But when,
in that letter, he went on to spell his answer out in words,
it was not an answer made of words: it was an answer
made of life: "When I try to put it all into a phrase I say,
'Man can embody truth but he cannot know it.'" Which
means, to me at least, that man can *live* his truth, his deepest truth, but cannot speak it. It is for this reason that love
becomes the ultimate human answer to the ultimate human
question. Love, in reason's terms, answers nothing. We say
that *Amor vincit omnia* but in truth love conquers nothing
—certainly not death—certainly not chance. What love
does is to affirm. It affirms the worth of life in spite of life.
It affirms the wonder and the beauty of the human creature, mortal and insignificant and ignorant though he be.
It answers life with life and so justifies that bravely tolling
line of Shakespeare's that declares that love "bears it out
even to the edge of doom." Love does: and for us no less
than for that ancient man who took back his life again
after all that wretchedness. J. B., like Job, covers his mouth
with his hand; acquiesces in the vast indifference of the
universe as all men must who truly face it; takes back his
life again. In love. To live.

I suppose, if I am really to justify my trespass, I must go
on to say that, though human beings have taken back their
lives over and over, generation after generation since time
began, they have, perhaps, never done so with such desperate courage as in these past, strange years. Men, our own
contemporaries, have already sat as Job did on an earth
reduced to ash-heap, picking in agony at the cinders of a

bomb-scorched skin, asking Job's eternal question. We know that they have sat there. We know that we may sit there too. But we also know something more. We know that even men like these can learn, in Yeats's words, to "live it all again."

LORRAINE HANSBERRY

The Negro in the American Theatre

I WAS visited some weeks ago by a young actress, a member of the cast of a quite successful Broadway show, who had herself won considerable praise from critics and audiences. I also knew her to be among the truly serious students of her profession: one of those devoted actors who spend so many self-imposed extra hours per week in dance, acting, and voice studios. She was twenty-four, deeply talented, profoundly dedicated to her work, possessed of a vigorous Broadway credit, and—a Negro.

So we spoke at length of her career. Had she, for instance, had offers of other work when the current show closed? "Well," she told me between two sighs, "there is a fall-coming show that I was called in to read for. It turned out to be an opportunity to play Young Negro Problem again." She explained discerningly that an American author, on the incomplete, if desperately welcome, rebound from stereotypes, had written a part for someone who was to make an entrance as a Social Question and exit as a Social Question. And that swiftly.

"How," she asked, "can anybody study for *that?* How can you find shading and character in the absence of shading and character?" As an actress she wanted to know how it was possible to interpret humanly that which was simply devoid of human definition. When would contemporary dramatists not be afraid to invest Negro characters with ordinary human complication, now that, to some degree, more overtly obnoxious traditions had started to fade?

First published under the title "Me Tink Me Hear Sounds in de Night," in *Theatre Arts*, XLIV (October, 1960), 9–10, 69–70, and reprinted here with the permission of Rembar & Zolotar.

Thinking of her excellent notices in the current show, I asked if what she had described had *really* been the only sign of future work. She laughed and replied, "Oh, no. I had a television call to read for a *traditional*. Not a maid; the *other* category, the 'native girl' bit. And, thought I, a job is a job. So I got the script, studied the lines, and went to the reading. And I read: *'Me sit on me hummock and me tink me hear sounds in de night and den . . .'* I finally just choked up on it, and closed the book and thanked the people for hearing me, and left. I just can't make that scene any more, my dear. Dis here native is tired of sittin' on de hummock!"

When she departed I was left to reflect on the general situation of Negroes in the American theatre. The authors of the two plays we had discussed were not singularly stupid or untalented people; the question was larger and deeper than their mere inadequacy in dealing with certain kinds of characterization. They had been trapped creatively by an old, monumentally encompassing, and deeply entrenched legacy from history.

The sixteenth-century spirit of mercantile expansionism that swept Europe, and gave rise to colonial conquest and the European slave trade, was also father of a modern concept of racism. The concept made it possible to render the African a "commodity" in the minds of white men, and to alienate the conscience of the rising European humanism from identification with the victims of that conquest and slave trade. In order to accommodate programs of commerce and empire on a scale never before known in history, the Negro had to be placed arbitrarily outside the pale of recognizable humanity in the psychology of Europeans and, eventually, of white America. Neither his soul nor his body was to be allowed to evoke empathy. He was to be—and, indeed, *became,* in a created mentality of white men—some grotesque expression of the mirth of nature; a fancied static vestige of the primeval past; an eternal exotic who, unlike men, would not bleed when pricked nor revenge when wronged. Thus for three centuries in Europe and America alike, buffoonery or villainy was his only permissible role in the hall of entertainment or drama. And notwithstanding the few later exceptions in Europe (the most distinguished, of course, being the career of Ira Aldridge, an American-born Negro actor of the nineteenth century who toured Europe in Shakespearean companies and achieved considerable recognition), in America the sight or even the notion of a Negro gripped in the complex agonies of a Hamlet outraged a cultural legend as today it yet embarrasses it.

That is why, 140 years ago, local hoodlums descended on the African Repertory Theatre Company at Bleecker and Mercer Streets in New York City, and harassed its actors and audiences out of existence. And that is why Negroes are not integrated in our theatre today.

It is this old historical situation that confronts a theatre, some of whose dramatists are currently baffled by Negro character, and whose producers and their receptionists are reduced to rudeness or apologetic embarrassment as they face the miraculously stubborn and increasing battalion of dark, hopeful faces among the multitude of other hopeful faces in their famous outer offices.

Presumably talent, all talent, is good for the theatre as democracy is for a democratic nation. But to say so is to ignore that breathlessness and perplexed expression in the countenance of our theatre as it asks, over and over again, "What can *realistically* be done about integrating the Negro in the theatre, given the present racial climate in the United States?"

The question implies that to integrate Negro actors in most dramatic situations is to perpetrate a social lie and invalidate the responsibility of art. It also has a way of starting at the point where artistic questions *are* relevant. It rather sneakingly ignores a stupendous area where "art" has nothing to do with discrimination in the theatre. For instance, I have never had the experience of purchasing a ticket from a Negro in a Broadway box office; I cannot imagine it to be a matter of either art or qualification, since, I can testify from personal experience, short-temperedness is not limited to white people, and it is that trait, we have all come to assume, that is the prime qualification for those legendary posts. Nor have I ever purchased a box of mints, or received my program, from a Negro lobby vendor or usher. And, to proceed to more important areas,

I have not, in my wanderings backstage, found my 10 per
cent represented in the handling of flats, lights, or properties, or calling time to the actors. Only on the rarest of
occasions have I spotted Negroes in the orchestra pits (I
believe only at New York's City Center does that phenomenon occur with even minimal regularity); and never, of
course, wielding the baton, despite the lingering legend of
a certain people's acute "musicalbility." Similar observations may be made of the chorus lines in our musical
comedies.

As for the situation among other echelons of the theatre
—the actors, writers, and directors—I think only the first
two deserve more concentrated thought than the categories
already covered. Directors should be men or women who
are sufficiently talented to have works of art put under
their direction. I cannot believe that their height, diet,
place of birth, or race will affect those talents. Naturally
it is to be desired that a director have adequate cultural
reference to his script, but intelligence dictates that we do
not hesitate to appoint plays with Japanese settings to
Americans, or American settings to decidedly English directors, and so on. When they are good directors they
direct well; when they are poor ones they direct poorly. I
have never been able to tell by the quality of a mounting
what kind of accent a director has; only whether or not he
has done a professional and imaginative piece of work. It
would, indeed, take an imaginative piece of argument to
show how or why it should be different for Negro directors.

The question of the employment of Negro actors, however, does raise interesting questions, which, it may be
argued, in a different sociological atmosphere would be
only minor questions of production techniques. But at the
moment a fascinating and revealing dichotomy exists within
the theatre's most literate circles with regard to the use of
Negro actors. People who are most bored and outraged by
what they call Ibsenesque or Shavian "boxes" on the imagination of the contemporary theatre, who long for fancy
and illusion to take utter command, who can deliver whole
sermons on the Philistinism of breaking "real eggs" on
stage, very often are, astonishingly enough, among the first
to shout betrayal of "realistic" attitudes if one speaks of

putting a Negro actor into a non-Negro role. It is most curious. Whoever said, for instance, that Queen Titania was white—or anything else? Or the incidental postman, policeman, clerk, or schoolmate in that contemporary play? Or *all* the people in that New York City crowd scene that is allegedly in Times Square. It takes rather more of a trick to imagine a good many urban American scenes without Negroes than with them.

But, above all, to defend a color barrier in the theatre is to ignore or argue against its essence, which has always been illusion. We do not get the blind to play the blind, or infants to play infants. Nor do we move Southern mansions or oceans on stage. It is not necessary. Our theatre must attain a sufficient degree of maturity and sophistication to put aside artificial barriers, to acknowledge that any truly qualified actor, Negro or white, who is made up properly, can do the job. I am speaking, of course, of roles that specify particular skin and hair coloring. When such matters are irrelevant rather than intrinsic, they should be viewed for what they are, and not be made the imagined basis for such barriers.

With regard to Negro writers, the theatre is yet saddled with the notion that their materials are necessarily parochial, and consequently without interest to the general theatregoing public. It is a difficult attitude to prove by looking back over the last six or seven years, when a fast total of *three* scripts by Negro writers was allowed to reach the Broadway stage for judgment by the *public*. It is interesting to note that of the three, two were quite first-rate efforts. The first found a steady and appreciative audience off Broadway when its Broadway run came to a close, and a subsequent motion-picture sale made a rather tidy sum for its investors. The second not only copped a prize, and earned over a million and a half at last count; it ran more than a year (an excellent record, in view of the disturbingly poor showings made by dramas these days), and got itself scheduled for national tour this season; it received production and translation throughout the world, and only its motion-picture production schedule prevented the American company from being sent abroad, as requested by our government, *to represent our national drama*. That is a peculiar kind of parochialism. And even the third show, a dreadful little piece, lasted several weeks too long, in my opinion, before it was buried. Viewed from any point of view, it is hardly a ratio that the rest of Broadway could duplicate.

The above should not be confused, as it often is, with the production of "Negro shows" by non-Negro writers, a somewhat different field. Such shows can be produced more easily, and they are in an area that requires the most revolutionary transition. In the theatre it is our dramatists and musical-comedy book writers who have the largest responsibility for presenting our world to us with ever-increasing penetration and illumination. Sad to say, they have, with only a few fine and notable exceptions, an exceedingly poor tradition to draw on with regard to Negroes because of the scale of the old alienation.

The Negro, as primarily presented in the past, has never existed on land or sea. It has seldom been a portrait of men, only a portrait of a concept, and that concept has been a romance and no other thing. By its very nature white supremacy longed for the contentment of the Negro with "his place"; one is always eager to believe that *somebody else* is exhilarated by "plenty of nuttin'." Since real-life Negroes—with their history of insurrection, "underground railways," mass enlistments in the Union army, petitions, delegations, organizations, press, and literature, and even music of protest—have failed to oblige, the white writer, in the main, has not failed to people *his* "Negro world" with Negroes who did not seem to know that slavery was intolerable, or that the subsequent and lingering oppression was a form of hell on earth. Thus in the make-believe domains of Porgy and Brutus Jones, only the foibles of *other Negroes* are assaulted; otherwise the heady passions of this particular happy breed are committed only to sex, liquor, and mysteriously motivated ultra-violence, usually over "dis or dat womans." A larger scale of dreams and anguish eluded their creators, and showed some otherwise great creative imaginations to be incapable of the recognition of the universal complexity of humankind.

This does not imply that malice has always been the intent. It would be as foolish to think that Mark Twain or

Mrs. Stowe tried to defeat their own humanist protests as to suppose that Marc Connelly, in a different vein, ever dreamed that he was writing a racist document in *The Green Pastures*. Rather, it is a matter of a partially innocent cultural heritage that, out of its own needs, was eager to believe in the colossal charm, among other things, of "childlike" peoples. From that notion, presumably, came the tendency to find non-Negro dramatic and musical materials rendered "quaint" when performed by "all-colored casts." From such an astonishing idea we have been treasured with the likes of *Carmen Jones* in the past, and will undoubtedly be treated to something like *Honeychile Tosca* in the future before it is exhausted. It is also interesting to note, in view of the hoped-for transition, that these translations "to the Negro" have generally meant (aside from adding saxophones and red dresses) haphazardly assaulting the English language beyond recognition, as if the Negro people had not produced an idiom that has a real and specific character, which is not merely the random exclusion of verb endings.

That does not suggest a counterdesire to see Negroes talking (or behaving) just like "everybody else" because, by and large, Negroes do no such thing, as conscientious playwrights will swiftly discover. And neither does "everybody else." American speech is as varied as the wind, and few of our sophisticated writers would dream of putting the speech of Texans into the mouths of New Yorkers for any purpose save that of the broadest comedy. So there is nothing extraordinary in the expectation that Negro speech must eventually be presented with artistic respect for its true color, nuances, and variations as they exist for each class and generation.

Finally, I think that American writers have already begun to believe what I suspect has always been one of the secrets of fine art: that there are no simple men. Chinese peasants and Congolese soldiers make drastic revolutions in the world while the obtuse and myth-accepting go on reflecting on the "inscrutability and eternal placidity" of those people. I believe that when the blinders are dropped, it will be discovered that while an excessively poignant Porgy was being instilled in generations of Americans, his truer-life counterpart was ravaged by longings that were, and are, in no way alien to those of the rest of mankind, and that bear within them the stuff of truly great art. He is waiting yet for those of us who will but look more carefully into his eyes, and listen more intently to his soliloquies. We must not be intimidated by the residue of the past; the world is paying too large a price for the deception of those centuries; each hour that flies teaches that Porgy is as much inclined to hymns of sedition as to lullabies and love songs; he is profoundly complicated and interesting; everywhere he is making his own sounds in the night. I believe that it is within the cultural descendants of Twain and Whitman and Melville and O'Neill to listen and absorb them, along with the totality of the American landscape, and give back their findings in new art to the great and vigorous institution that is the American theatre.

EDWARD ALBEE

Which Theatre Is the Absurd One?

A THEATRE PERSON of my acquaintance—a man whose judgment must be respected, though more for the infallibility of his intuition than for his reasoning—remarked just the other week, "The Theatre of the Absurd has had it; it's on its way out; it's through."

Now this, on the surface of it, seems to be a pretty funny attitude to be taking toward a theatre movement which has, only in the past couple of years, been impressing itself on the American public consciousness. Or is it? Must we judge that a theatre of such plays as Samuel Beckett's *Krapp's Last Tape,* Jean Genet's *The Balcony* (both long, long runners off-Broadway) and Eugène Ionesco's *Rhinoceros*—which, albeit in a hoked-up production, had a substantial season *on* Broadway—has been judged by the theatre public and found wanting?

And shall we have to assume that The Theatre of the Absurd Repertory Company, currently playing at New York's off-Broadway Cherry Lane Theatre—presenting works by Beckett, Ionesco, Genet, Arrabal, Jack Richardson, Kenneth Koch, and myself—being the first such collective representation of the movement in the United States, is also a kind of farewell to the movement? For that matter, just what *is* The Theatre of the Absurd?

Well, let me come at it obliquely. When I was told, about a year ago, that I was considered a member in good standing of The Theatre of the Absurd I was deeply offended. I was deeply offended because I had never heard

First published in *The New York Times Magazine* of February 25, 1962, and reprinted here by permission of William Morris Agency, Inc.

the term before and I immediately assumed that it applied
to the theatre uptown—Broadway.

What (I was reasoning to myself) could be more absurd
than a theatre in which the esthetic criterion is something
like this: A "good" play is one which makes money; a
"bad" play (in the sense of "Naughty! Naughty!" I guess)
is one which does not; a theatre in which performers have
plays rewritten to correspond to the public relations image
of themselves; a theatre in which playwrights are encouraged (what a funny word!) to think of themselves as
little cogs in a great big wheel; a theatre in which imitation
has given way to imitation of imitation; a theatre in which
London "hits" are, willy-nilly, in a kind of reverse of
chauvinism, greeted in a manner not unlike a colony's
obeisance to the Crown; a theatre in which real estate owners and theatre party managements predetermine the success of unknown quantities; a theatre in which everybody
scratches and bites for billing as though it meant access to
the last bomb shelter on earth; a theatre in which, in a
given season, there was not a single performance of a play
by Beckett, Brecht, Chekhov, Genet, Ibsen, O'Casey, Piran-
dello, Shaw, Strindberg—or Shakespeare? What, indeed, I
thought, could be more absurd than that? (My conclusions . . . obviously.)

For it emerged that The Theatre of the Absurd, aside
from being the title of an excellent book by Martin Esslin
on what is loosely called the avant-garde theatre, was a
somewhat less than fortunate catch-all phrase to describe
the philosophical attitudes and theatre methods of a number of Europe's finest and most adventurous playwrights
and their followers.

I was less offended, but still a little dubious. Simply: I
don't like labels; they can be facile and can lead to non-
think on the part of the public. And unless it is understood
that the playwrights of The Theatre of the Absurd represent a group only in the sense that they seem to be doing
something of the same thing in vaguely similar ways at ap-
proximately the same time—unless this is understood, then
the labeling itself will be more absurd than the label.

Playwrights, by nature, are grouchy, withdrawn, envious,
greedy, suspicious and, in general, quite nice people—and

the majority of them wouldn't be caught dead in a colloquy remotely resembling the following:

IONESCO (*At a Left Bank café table, spying Beckett and Genet strolling past in animated conversation*): Hey! Sam! Jean!

GENET: Hey, it's Eugene! Sam, it's Eugene!

BECKETT: Well, I'll be damned. Hi there, Eugene boy.

IONESCO: Sit down, kids.

GENET: Sure thing.

IONESCO (*Rubbing his hands together*): Well, what's new in The Theatre of the Absurd?

BECKETT: Oh, less than a lot of people think. (*They all laugh.*)

Etc. No. Not very likely. Get a playwright alone sometime, get a few drinks in him, and maybe he'll be persuaded to sound off about his "intention" and the like—and hate himself for it the next day. But put a group of playwrights together in a room, and the conversation—if there is any —will, more likely than not, concern itself with sex, restaurants, and the movies.

Very briefly, then—and reluctantly, because I am a playwright and would much rather talk about sex, restaurants, and the movies—and stumblingly, because I do not pretend to understand it entirely, I will try to define The Theatre of the Absurd. As I get it, The Theatre of the Absurd is an absorption-in-art of certain existentialist and post-existentialist philosophical concepts having to do, in the main, with man's attempts to make sense for himself out of his senseless position in a world which makes no sense—which makes no sense because the moral, religious, political, and social structures man has erected to "illusion" himself have collapsed.

Albert Camus put it this way: "A world that can be explained by reasoning, however faulty, is a familiar world. But in a universe that is suddenly deprived of illusions and of light, man feels a stranger. His is an irremediable exile, because he is deprived of memories of a lost homeland as much as he lacks the hope of a promised land to come.

This divorce between man and his life, the actor and his setting, truly constitutes the feeling of Absurdity."

And Eugène Ionesco says this: "Absurd is that which is devoid of purpose. . . . Cut off from his religious, metaphysical, and transcendental roots, man is lost; all his actions become senseless, absurd, useless."

And to sum up the movement, Martin Esslin writes, in his book *The Theatre of the Absurd:* "Ultimately, a phenomenon like The Theatre of the Absurd does not reflect despair or a return to dark irrational forces but expresses modern man's endeavor to come to terms with the world in which he lives. It attempts to make him face up to the human condition as it really is, to free him from illusions that are bound to cause constant maladjustment and disappointment. . . . For the dignity of man lies in his ability to face reality in all its senselessness; to accept it freely, without fear, without illusions—and to laugh at it."

Amen.

(And while we're on the subject of Amen, one wearies of the complaint that The Theatre of the Absurd playwrights alone are having at God these days. The notion that God is dead, indifferent, or insane—a notion blasphemous, premature, or academic depending on your persuasion—while surely a tenet of some of the playwrights under discussion, is, it seems to me, of a piece with Mr. Tennessee Williams' description of the Deity, in *The Night of the Iguana,* as "a senile delinquent.")

So much for the attempt to define terms. Now, what of this theatre? What of this theatre in which, for example, a legless old couple live out their lives in twin ashcans, surfacing occasionally for food or conversation (Samuel Beckett's *Endgame*); in which a man is seduced, and rather easily, by a girl with three well-formed and functioning noses (Eugène Ionesco's *Jack, or The Submission*); in which, on the same stage, one group of Negro actors is playing at pretending to be Negro (Jean Genet's *The Blacks*)?

What of this theatre? Is it, as it has been accused of being, obscure, sordid, destructive, anti-theatre, perverse, and absurd (in the sense of foolish)? Or is it merely, as I have so often heard it put, that, "This sort of stuff is too depressing, too . . . too mixed-up; I go to the theatre to relax and have a good time."

I would submit that it is this latter attitude—that the theatre is a place to relax and have a good time—in conflict with the purpose of The Theatre of the Absurd—which is to make a man face up to the human condition as it really is—that has produced all the brouhaha and the dissent. I would submit that The Theatre of the Absurd, in the sense that it is truly the contemporary theatre, facing as it does man's condition as it is, is the Realistic theatre of our time; and that the supposed Realistic theatre—the term used here to mean most of what is done on Broadway —in the sense that it panders to the public need for self-congratulation and reassurance and presents a false picture of ourselves to ourselves, is, with an occasional very lovely exception, really and truly The Theatre of the Absurd.

And I would submit further that the health of a nation, a society, can be determined by the art it demands. We have insisted of television and our movies that they not have anything to do with anything, that they be our never-never land; and if we demand this same function of our live theatre, what will be left of the visual-auditory arts— save the dance (in which nobody talks) and music (to which nobody listens)?

It has been my fortune, the past two or three years, to travel around a good deal, in pursuit of my career—Berlin, London, Buenos Aires, for example; and I have discovered a couple of interesting things. I have discovered that audiences in these and other major cities demand of their commercial theatre—and get—a season of plays in which the froth and junk are the exception and not the rule. To take a case: in Berlin, in 1959, Adamov, Genet, Beckett, and Brecht (naturally) were playing the big houses; this past fall, Beckett again, Genet again, Pinter twice, etc. To take another case: in Buenos Aires there are over a hundred experimental theatres.

These plays cannot be put on in Berlin over the head of a protesting or an indifferent audience; these experimental theatres cannot exist in Buenos Aires without subscription.

In the end—and it must always come down to this, no matter what other failings a theatre may have—in the end a public will get what it deserves, and no better.

I have also discovered, in my wanderings, that young people throng to what is new and fresh in the theatre. Happily, this holds true in the United States as well. At the various colleges I have gone to to speak I have found an eager, friendly, and knowledgeable audience, an audience which is as dismayed by the Broadway scene as any proselytizer for the avant-garde. I have found among young people an audience which is not so preconditioned by pap as to have cut off half of its responses. (It is interesting to note, by the way, that if an off-Broadway play has a substantial run, its audiences will begin young and grow older; as the run goes on, cloth coats give way to furs, walkers and subway riders to taxi-takers. Exactly the opposite is true on Broadway.)

The young, of course, are always questioning values, knocking the status quo about, considering shibboleths to see if they are pronounceable. In time, it is to be regretted, most of them—the kids—will settle down to their own version of the easy, the standard; but in the meanwhile . . . in the meanwhile they are a wonderful, alert, alive, accepting audience.

And I would go so far as to say that it is the responsibility of everyone who pretends any interest at all in the theatre to get up off their six-ninety seats and find out what the theatre is *really* about. For it is a lazy public which produces a slothful and irresponsible theatre.

Now, I would suspect that my theatre-friend with the infallible intuition is probably right when he suggests that The Theatre of the Absurd (or the avant-garde theatre, or whatever you want to call it) as it now stands is on its way out. Or at least is undergoing change. All living organisms undergo constant change. And while it is certain that the nature of this theatre will remain constant, its forms, its methods—its devices, if you will—most necessarily will undergo mutation.

This theatre has no intention of running downhill; and the younger playwrights will make use of the immediate past and mold it to their own needs. (Harold Pinter, for example, could not have written *The Caretaker* had Samuel Beckett not existed, but Pinter is, nonetheless, moving in his own direction.) And it is my guess that the theatre in the United States will always hew more closely to the post-Ibsen/Chekhov tradition than does the theatre in France, let us say. It is our nature as a country, a society. But we will experiment, and we will expect your attention.

For just as it is true that our response to color and form was forever altered once the impressionist painters put their minds to canvas, it is just as true that the playwrights of The Theatre of the Absurd have forever altered our response to the theatre.

And one more point: The avant-garde theatre is fun; it is free-swinging, bold, iconoclastic, and often wildly, wildly funny. If you will approach it with childlike innocence—putting your standard responses aside, for they do not apply—if you will approach it on its own terms, I think you will be in for a liberating surprise. I think you may no longer be content with plays that you can't remember halfway down the block. You will not only be doing yourself some good, but you will be having a great time, to boot. And even though it occurs to me that such a fine combination must be sinful, I still recommend it.